Praise for What Color Is Your Soul?

"Building a more just and equitable world is a matter of policy and a just distribution of power. It is also a challenge of the spirit. In *What Color Is Your Soul?* Niambi Jaha-Echols writes an artful meditation on the healing work that humans must do to overcome our brutal history and our deep divisions, especially those resulting from centuries of white supremacy. We must transform ourselves, collectively and individually, and this book offers a call to that work."

~ John Biewen, host and producer, Scene on Radio podcast

"In this wonderfully engaging book, Niambi Jaha-Echols offers her unique, expansive and well-supported perspective on racism in America. Not only how we found our way into our current situation but also encouragement to remove our blinders, accept personal responsibility and take fruitful action to bring mutual respect, understanding and harmony into our culture. Niambi weaves her personal story throughout the book giving it an air of authenticity and personal commitment. An exciting, thought-provoking, heart-opening journey - a great read!"

~ John S. Shealy, PhD, psychotherapist and life coach
(www.BeMindful.org)

"This book is amazing. There are many wonderful aspects to it, as analogies, personal experiences, and the use of pearls of wisdom in quotes are woven eloquently throughout. It's an easy read and easy to digest, with something in it for everyone depending on where you are in your self-awareness."

~ MaryAnne Howland, founder & CEO, Ibis Communications
(www.ibiscommunications.com)

"From the very beginning I was hooked. The ancestral story of Akna told a different tale than what many have come to believe. It is time for a conscious, global color conversation. "What Color is your Soul" is a Wake Up

Call for a society where Colorism is a daily, passive aggressive form of racism turned inside out. As stated by Ms. Jaha-Echols, "Colorism is baked into the very fibers of our cultural tapestries and is wrapped in our psyches. "What a TRUE Gift and breath of fresh air for a higher vibration conversation!"
~ Tonya R. Gonzalez, author, healer & teacher
(www.tonyargonzalez.com)

"You have exceptional insight and knowledge about the subject matter and an inspiration for others of any cultural background. In a world of multiculturalism, there's still ignorance about culture, race, women, social norms. As a child growing up in the 60s near Detroit, I experienced a lot in the changing linear society they thought was truth, but then the civil rights days came, and helped to make a change in how American society viewed it's ever growing cultural and multiculturalism movements. I love your presentation in how you tell your story! Coming from the past and our Native ancestors, Collective nature of beings can still be taught to synthesize the needed connectiveness of the human soul from which we all came from. All of this is temporary and we should try to educate ourselves to correcting some really deep hurts in our connected souls to help the next generations, and you're doing it! Thank you."
~ Dr. Jiiniikwe Medicine Bird, Native music artist and actress

"Niambi's book begins the journey of introspection, exploring stories that shape our perceptions and unite cultures. As our knowledge changes through the world wide web, our consciousness weaves together, remnants of family. This author unravels roots of dissension, planting seeds of respect that bloom as you read."
~ Nancy Basket, artist & storyteller (www.nancybasket.com)

"Being 'woke' or socially aware is really just the beginning, Niambi Jaha-Echols explains in What Color is Your Soul? What's required is heart-work, ancestral healing and continual vigilance to see beyond the illusion of separation that ghettoizes us into silos of difference."
~ Angelo John Lewis, Director of the Diversity and Spirituality Network and author of Notes for a New Age

"*Reading the words that Niambi wrote is like going back in time and feeling the emotions that my ancestors felt and in particular the women of my lineage. As an Intuitive Healer, the level that we vibrate at is something I think about daily. I resonate with the way that Niambi speaks about vibration. She articulates it in a way that anyone could understand that our stories, beliefs, emotions, circumstances, situations and thoughts carry a vibration that creates our reality. Niambi's words evoke emotion that fuels my soul to heal at the deepest level. It is only when I go within to heal, that I can begin to connect with a person on a soul level. Throughout reading* What Color Is Your Soul, *Niambi's message as I read it is healing myself all the way back to my roots' which requires me to go within and connect with what my soul is sharing with me. Reading Niambi's book brings a deeper awareness to the healing, cross culturally that still needs to happen. As I heal the deeper parts of myself, I open up to a culture of people that I maybe I felt distant from in the past. Thank you for such a thought provoking, soul nourishing book Niambi.*"

~ Tracy Neely, healer, priestess, and mentor (www.tracyneeley.com)

"*The book hit home in lots of ways. Starting with an eye opening story and perspective,* What Color is Your Soul?, *addresses the depth of what the color of our skin represents and why. With thoughtful, well written views spanning history and many beliefs, Niambi takes us through the difficult parts of our culture and into what can be done about it. Opening hearts and minds to the understanding of what issues we face every day is only the beginning, she provides the antidote too! By outlining how we can each develop our own ways of releasing ancestral patterns, Niambi leads us to a new way, to a new world, absent of racial inequality and unrest. There were parts of this book that made me uncomfortable because the truth of the words are, at times, deep and unsettling. Taking a raw look at the collective consciousness around race on our planet helped me see just how much we are all connected and how we can, together, make our Earth a better place.*"

~ Jason Antalek Akashaman, (www.thespiritualhandyman.com)

"*Earth herself is in motion to a new age, a new light, and is warming. We human Beings can feel this temperature within as well as our parasitic evolution is riding heavy and swiftly with the weight of our 'Human Condition' and the speed of our technological advances. The global computer age has delivered volumes of real-time libraries of information to the doorsteps of almost every person in the world. The imagery and written and spoken word of knowledge once hidden, great cultural manipulations, false histories and reclaimed histories, and illusion of separateness in our human role on the planet can be studied in almost every language. With so much access and transparency in our era, the potential for increased personal and cultural awareness is vast. If we want to activate and integrate and realize into our evolution at the pace of our advances or to the approaching light of Earth's passage, we must do the real work, the unlearning, the new learning, and the authentic living of what we are becoming aware of now. Talking and tryouts and sending thoughts and prayers are not going to keep up with the river of life moving so wide and fast right now. Niambi Jaha-Echols is nudging us into the real work that comes from educated 'awareness' and it reminds us that after you open your 'woke' eyes in the morning, one actually has to get out of bed and move in the world. This means opening one's mind to other ways of life than one's own, that our dated beliefs may not be true. This means opening one's heart to feel the pain of what has been lost to ignorance and manipulation, dominance and suppression, and to the fears that have led to so much greed and destruction. When I do this work personally from within and apply it, it merges locally, culturally, and globally. This book reminds me that it happens in that order."*

~ Aaron Ortega

"I cried while reading this book as it presented me with the space to do some deep healing ... and not just for myself, my ancestors too. It's amazing, really, the narratives that run our lives that we aren't even aware of. This book, if you allow it, will help you become aware of the stories around race and culture that have become dominant beliefs and will shift your narrative to one that is empowering ...one that more accurately reflects the Truth of who we all are: One."

~ DeAnna Carpenter, singer, songwriter, She Who Builds (www.dellesings.com)

WHAT COLOR IS YOUR SOUL?

HEALING THE ILLUSION OF OUR SEPARATENESS

NIAMBI JAHA-ECHOLS

Earth Light Publishing

Earth Light Publishing
2334 Millikan Road
Chapel Hill, NC 27516
www.NiambiJaha.com

Cover art: ©Agsandrew I Dreamstime.com
Cover & Interior Design: Publishing Shack (www.PublishingShack.com)

Ordering Information:
Quantity sales. Special discounts are available on quantity purchases by corporations, associations, and others. For details, contact the "Special Sales Department" at the address above.

What Color Is Your Soul?/ Niambi Jaha-Echols. -- 1st ed.
ISBN 978-0-9720854-5-8

ACKNOWLEDGEMENTS

Many thanks to all those who have helped in the development of this book, either by discussing their own experiences with me or by sharing their own understanding and insights. Gratitude and love are extended especially to the following: Jacque Anderson-Williams, Jamilah Sabir-Calloway, Sheila 'Iya Andito' Fairey, Zenobia Finney, Nancy Basket and Vandorn Hinnant.

Special thank you to Edith "Mama Edie" McLoud Armstrong my Contributing Editor for *The Story of Akna and Her Children*. Your love and energy is imprinted in the very fibers of the story. I am excited for all that will be birthed because of it. Thank you to Lynnclaire Dennis for your editorial encouragement as echoes of your voice rang through the book in its early stages. Thank you to DeAnna Carpenter for being the Editorial Midwife I needed to push through. Whispers of you fill every page. Thank you to Dr. Carmen Carter my Copy Editor for applying your detailed focus and expertise, getting this book project successfully to the finish line. Thank you to Kivoli and Publishing Shack for your design expertise and making sure that the book's cover and interior was better than anything I could have imagined (www.PublishingShack.com).

Thank you to Sisterfriend Marie McCohnell and Bonnie Hill for holding sacred space for safe and clear passage of this book and your encouragement and support every step of the way.

Finally, thank you to my husband Rod for all you do in love, collaboration and support of what I do, and to our son Jelani for giving me the time and space to work this all out.

Lastly, eternal gratitude to Divine Mother, all of my ancestors and my Collective Spiritual Posse' – too many and vast to name - thank you for your unwavering love, inspiration and support throughout this project, this lifetime, and forever more.

*Dedicated to all the colorful souls who are
beginning to remember.*

CONTENTS

FOREWORD

❖❖❖❖❖

This paragraph is a prelude to the Foreword, a personal perspective echoing what Niambi courageously shares in her invitation to engage an exploration of color, body, and soul. My thoughts come from love and are fueled by compassion, and my desire that what she shares inspires you to accept her invitation to take part in positive change. Read her words knowing in advance that doing so requires courage to understand and the willingness to harness emotions that will most certainly rise up to pull you in. My prayer is her thoughts will lift you to a new perspective, the place where points of light unexpectedly illumine things both ancient and new within you. Read knowing what inspires you has the power to open remembrance, igniting the inner peace that turns on your light and lights up the path you share with others.

Several weeks after sharing her manuscript, '*What Color Is Your Soul?*', Niambi and I enjoyed an energetic cyber-romp; a long and meaningful transatlantic call ending with her inviting me to write this Foreword. Hanging up the phone, plunging back into the sometimes deafening silence of my home, the hush didn't last long. Reflecting on Niambi's life and what she shared about her 'why' for writing this book led to a syntax storm of thoughts inside my head. The word "Foreword" turning into "forward" as it pin-balled inside my brain. When "forward" banged into the word "color", memories sparked, and the energy of the collision smacked into the other side where it hit the word "soul" who yelled and whacked it back. What began in North Carolina was a catalyst for dreams in Spain. Our emails, photographs, and text to one another began braiding a bridge across the Atlantic. As appreciation for our connection grew, we discovered how few strands of diversity were actually woven through our collective formative years. Those strands of difference, we found, were tenuous, thin and at best worn.

While our early life lessons were marked by differences; deep resonances echoed between them and were carried into adulthood. They then were mutually manifested in our mature and unwavering commitment to conscious co-creation (and the need for cooperation), to bring about positive change, facilitating human evolution, through body and spirit. I saw how our differences and seeming paradoxes were resolved time and again through the vibrant rainbow path we share. A true Love Knot!

"What Color Is Your Soul?" is filled with memories that led toinsight Niambi gleaned while living and mastering the skills necessary to help her and others navigate the layers of their lives. Living her quest, she strives to help you realize how living from authenticity begins inside and grows outward. Using the scientific evidence of our inner-and interconnection, she dares us to identify and unmask the existential lies we tell ourselves. She cares enough to recognize, own and heal her bias, knowing that doing so is the first step forward, the only direction we can move to heal the divisive bigotry hidden in plain sight in so many of our 'ities', 'isms', 'osophies' and 'ologies'. The moral imperative of this book is to remember and respond, re-membering essential to a sustainable connection with ourselves, our Source, and others.

Read *"What Color Is Your Soul?"* with the sole intent of understanding and fences will fall as the Field of Consciousness opens. Step into this space and you will experience how acceptance opens a previously unimaginable connection, letting you appreciate and mend the richly textured strands of diversity that weave unity's rainbow. The butterfly is a symbolic icon for both Niambi and I. More than a metaphor for the inner process of growth that leads to transformation, it reminds us that caterpillars who become butterflies don't have to take flying lessons. They simply remember and take flight. May Niambi's story help you find the colors that illumine possibilities that are true for you. May you find the vibration that frees your body, opens your heart and lifts you into the light of remembrance. May you fill your palette, awakening from the collective forgetfulness to join in the joy of TranscenDance.

~ Lynnclaire Dennis, Co-Founder of The Mereon Legacy CIC

A REMEMBRANCE: THE STORY OF AKNA AND HER CHILDREN

*If you know the entire story, you won't
get scared at the scary parts.*

Healing is in our stories: the stories we listen to, the stories we create, the scary stories we choose to frighten ourselves and our children with. Stories can contain medicine or poison; and when reading a book, many typically won't stop reading just because they've approached a particularly scary chapter. They're curious enough to want to know more, even with the threat of being made to feel excitedly afraid.

The greatest stories have drama for contrast, are layered with complexity, conflict, suspense, humor, love, fear, and surprise – all designed to keep the reader engaged because it's hard to resist a great story.

The additional inclusion of color and hue contribute vibrancy and depth, providing richness to any story. So, when someone says, *"I don't see color,"* when referring to people, it's like asserting that they are colorblind by choice. When one chooses not to see color in anything, parts of the image disappear, fading into the background or very likely were never even seen at all. It's noticing the spaces between the white on a canvas that makes the picture fascinating, just as it is the ink on a blank page that creates interest or at least arouses one's curiosity.

So, I'd like to share with you a very colorful story. It is a story told through the spirit of my ancestors. It is a story that will, hopefully, open up new perspectives that go beyond our typical red, black and white paradigm. Perhaps it will guide us into conversations that delve deeper into considerations that explore more than just the color of our skin.

THE STORY OF AKNA AND HER CHILDREN

"Why do they hate us so deeply?"
the children asked.

One could answer that question in many ways. In order to tell this tale, we have to travel back to an ancient time. It is a tale of one people who became many. In the process, they forgot who they were and their connection to each other. In the end, it will truly be one of the greatest love stories ever told.

This is the story of beloved Akna, as told through the eyes of her two older siblings: Aftab the Sun, Nokomis the Moon and Akna herself. Each one of us knows a part of this story and together are better able to connect, understand and relay with accuracy more of the whole. But for now, let the story begin...

Akna and her siblings gathered the children around them to tell them the story of why the spirit of hatred was so often hurled against them by others of their own relations. But the children had to be carefully taught. The desire was for them to better understand their relations and to not be inspired to hurl the hatred back against the others out of anger or revenge.

And so with Aftab the Sun, the story began: "The ALL (also known as Great Spirit) decided to make children in their image and likeness. But where would these children be placed? In their infancy, they had to grow somewhere. The request was sent out all across the Universe and our sister Akna answered the call."

Nokomis the Moon continued: "And Akna said, 'I will birth them. Mold them out of me and I will love, nurture and sustain them because they will indeed be my children.' The ALL agreed and it came to pass that in the land of AFAR, The ALL molded and shaped the children out of Akna's resources. At first, they were mere colorless, inanimate figures until The ALL breathed life into them, creating both male and female. They moved, worked, played and loved."

The ALL then spoke to Akna: "They will always be a part of you sweet Akna, because they will dwell on you and with you. They will suckle on your fruits and bounty. But how will they know me?" To address this matter, The ALL decided to place within each being a hidden eye. The two physical eyes allowed them to see Akna with her abundant and variable beauty; but also placed within them was a Spirit Eye – right above and between each being's physical eyes.

The Spirit Eye had many functions but primarily, it connected them back to The ALL. Through quieting their minds and closing their physical eyes, each could use the Spirit Eye to see and connect with this wondrous being. It was the most powerful way that they were able to connect with each other as well. Although they might not have always agreed, they were in-tuned to each other. They connected and lived together in ways that demonstrated that they cared about each other and sincerely wanted what was best for the whole. When all was said and done, they were family – and all was well.

Aftab, the Sun continued the story: "Another gift to maintain the connection with The ALL was the Elixir. It was a rich pigment that I helped to activate within the Spirit Eye. Once the powerful Elixir was activated, it would flow through one's entire being. At its fullest power, it illuminated the rich, beautiful, dark hue of Akna's children.

Nokomis, the Moon added: "The ALL and Akna were both quite pleased. The Elixir did amazing things to these now living and pulsating beings. As it coursed through their bodies, it deeply enhanced the rich color of their skin and eyes. Their hair rose in joyful coils, spiraling like antennae, reaching upward and outward toward the Universe."

Aftab, the Sun continued: "There were many hidden gifts as well. As the Elixir pulsed through the Spirit Eye, it helped the children to feel love and to truly know Akna and The ALL quite deeply. When they closed their eyes, everyone could see, and more importantly, they could feel the invisible connections between all living things. They could feel and recognize the rhythmic beat of Akna's heart as it pulsated through their bodies, and even through the soles of their bare feet. It provided the rhythm to which they worked, played, danced and sang. It inspired the rhythm to which they expressed their love. All living things that drew life from Akna's existence were connected to them. They were in harmony with her and with all of her wondrous creations."

As the siblings continued their story, they explained that all while the Elixir flowed through the newly created beings, they were revealed to be truly magnificent indeed. With The ALL and Akna as their source of life, an abundance of creativity, intelligence and power was theirs. The Elixir flowed through their bodies like blood – but it was something more. Its path flowed from the Spirit Eye, to the heart and then to the soul. Blood could not penetrate the soul. The Elixir within them became the vibratory frequency that broadcast from The ALL and to The ALL and throughout the whole Universe. The entire galactic family across this great vastness rejoiced and loved the new beings. They had such hope...

Akna's older brother Aftab, the Sun had vowed to stay close enough to Akna to keep the Elixir activated. His warm rays brought it to life. It was like an electrical current that kept this magnificent life force flowing. The brighter Aftab's light shown, the stronger the Elixir became.

Ignited by this force moving within her, Akna swayed, slowly dancing in rhythmic circles, the nature of which changed from season to season. Aftab could see his sister's energy being fueled by the Elixir. It enhanced the almost synaptic connections among all within their vibrational field and out into the Universe. Aftab beamed his brightest over the land of AFAR where the new beings were born. This place became their energy center.

Akna's older sister Nokomis, the Moon vowed to provide light as Akna danced so that anywhere that Aftab was not present, she would always be there to provide light in his shadow for Akna's children.

As they grew, the children had many questions. "Where is The ALL?" they asked.

"Everywhere," Akna replied, "even within you."

For certain ideas, Akna knew that it would take time and maturation for her children to more fully understand. But she always provided in ways that they could best comprehend the answers to every question. It would feed their souls and provide the knowledge that would sustain them. This was often done through story or song. Then the children were encouraged to create from the natural materials around them images that reflected their understanding of what they had been taught. They were also encouraged to re-tell the stories, to create songs, rhythms and dances reflecting the essence of these lessons. In this way, at the same time that this allowed the children to express their creativity, it also allowed Akna to stay in-tuned with them and she could monitor — and correct — the accuracy of their understanding.

"And why do we have bodies?" the young ones asked.

Akna explained: "So, that you can enjoy yourselves; so that, through your senses, you can enjoy me, and I you, and all of this creation. You have bodies so that you can explore, grow, create and love. The ALL is a vibration. When you close your eyes, breathe through your heart. Feel the pulse and rhythm of me you will remember that The ALL and we are one."

The story continued. It was explained by her siblings that as time passed, Akna bore more and more children with The ALL. Each new being was unique. While they were similar in many ways, no two were exactly the same. As Akna's family grew, many continued to live and to happily thrive in AFAR, while others explored in every direction. And why not? After all, there was nothing to fear. They explored Akna's mountains and valleys, her deserts and seas. What bound them all together was the rhythm and heartbeat of their Great Mother. She fed and sustained them as they ventured out. They peacefully parceled out land among each other upon which to build new homes. This worked well in most cases because they were mature enough to know how to share. They created families of their own and lived in love. They loved their Great Mother Akna. They were her beloved children. They knew that she loved them deeply and that wherever they ventured, she would provide food, shelter and engaging, even amusing experiences for them to enjoy. There was so much for them to learn, to create and to do that in their language there was no word for 'boredom.'

One day, Gramaldi, one of Akna's beloved daughters, decided to take her family to explore the far reaches of Akna. Gramaldi knew that her Great Mother would watch over them; she had no concerns. So, they traveled high into the Northeast Mountains. They were amazed with wonder at the difference of it all. Even the air they breathed was not quite the same. It was thinner, lighter. And it somehow suited Gramaldi and seemed quite natural to be so high above all else. Happy with the change in environment, Gramaldi and her children settled there. They were gone from AFAR for many, many years. But they always securely felt their connections to 'home' and the love of their Great Mother Akna.

While Gramaldi was in the mountains, however, Akna had somehow begun to change. Her various transitions began to affect life all around her. Something happened even within her. Parts of Akna's being had become extremely cold. Thick sheets of impenetrable ice covered segments of her great spherical body. The climatic shift happened so suddenly that Gramaldi and her family had no choice but to seek more secure shelter even higher in the mountain caves.

As the temperature continued to rapidly drop, Gramaldi and her family were trapped by the ice. They were isolated from the rest of Akna's children. Their rhythmic frequency, which would normally connect them to Akna's heartbeat, could not be felt because its weakened vibration was blocked by the humongous wall of ice that now separated them.

Gramaldi and her children cried out, "Mama Akna, why did this happen? Where are you? Why won't you save us?" But Akna could not respond.

Although she could not directly hear her daughter, Akna sensed Gramaldi's despair. She could only hold her dear one in love and send strength to Gramaldi in that love. She could only hope that the choices she made and what she had been taught about survival would keep her and her children safe. She hoped that The ALL would protect them.

Akna then reflected, "This entire sphere is my body, with its mountains, rivers, plants, and atmosphere. I have known many cycles – it is my process of evolution. I have been this way since the beginning of my beginning. This is how I grow and regenerate. I have always done this, for billions of years. This is how I am made. It is part of my internal system, just as one doesn't directly control the functioning of one's liver, kidneys or other organs within the body. Volcanoes, earthquakes and such are like that for me as well, and I have no direct control over them. When the ice rose from within, it had done that before, only before and all of the many 'befores,' there were no concerns. It came and eventually it left. The only difference this time was that I had given birth and my children were there in the mountain ice. I could not reach them, and they couldn't feel my vibration. I yearned for them. I cried for them. My spirit mourned for them. But they did not know. They didn't understand. How could they?"

The siblings explained that the ice was so thick that even Akna's brother Aftab, the Sun could not melt it. All Akna could do was to send her older sister Nokomis the Moon, to watch over Gramaldi as best she could, to at least provide a bit of light, to guide her in her darkest moments.

Aftab continued: "Nokomis tried her best to comfort Gramaldi and her children while they were separated in the icy mountain caves. Gramaldi was in shock and disbelief that neither Akna nor The ALL would help them! Their lives were extremely difficult. There was very little to eat and many of Gramaldi's children became ill and died. They had never had to fight so viciously with other animals and creatures simply to survive. They were all trapped and food was very scarce. Only the very strongest of Gramaldi's children were able to survive."

"Gramaldi tried to communicate with The ALL while in the caves," explained Nokomis. *"Without the strong rays of their uncle Aftab the Sun, the Elixir could not be activated. Over time the Elixir hardened, calcified and no longer flowed through them. Each one's Spirit Eye grew dim and eventually shut, just as one closes one's physical eyes to sleep. Without the Elixir, their facial and other bodily features, even their voices, began to change. Without the warming chemistry of the sun that kept their dark pigment strong, their skin became lighter and lighter. Without the protection of the Elixir, even their skin began to burn much more easily under the rays of the sun. Their eyes lost the beautiful dark hue that once reflected the peace of the night sky. Their hair lost its strong texture, its natural, joyful ascending coil. Instead it became limp as it loosely hung downward and turned the color and texture of straw. Gramaldi and her children fell into a dull, walking, sleep-like trance."*

Aftab continued: *"They could not believe that Akna and The ALL would betray them. Gramaldi just knew that Akna would come and rescue her! She knew how much her Great Mother loved her! Surely, she would send some of her siblings to rescue them. Surely someone would come! But no one came."*

"When the ice came and the Elixir calcified," said Nokomis the Moon, *"I tried to comfort Gramaldi and her children with my light. But now unable to feel the vibratory current of the Elixir flowing within her, she could not hear my words nor could she any longer feel her connections to the rest of the family. And with her Spirit Eye now closed, she could not see that, despite her despair, her mother Akna still loved her and mourned for her. All I could do was to comfort her as best I could with my presence. I listened as Gramaldi would tell her children that her mother Akna would come for them; that The ALL would come for them. And when neither came, Gramaldi grew extremely angry. Her heart began to turn as ice cold as her surroundings. She started planting seeds of bitterness and hatred towards Akna within her children. She told them to never forget this gross betrayal*

and abandonment. She vowed that neither she nor her surviving children would be cold, desolate or without ever again. With this hatred planted deep in the souls of her children, each generation that survived the harsh isolation nurtured this bitterness until it had festered for thousands of years. As time passed, because of their cold surroundings, they became increasingly more comfortable in colder temperatures than in those that warmed their skin. Their emotions and sensitivity to others reflected this reality as they became colder as well.

Akna's siblings continued to explain that after many thousands of years, the story of Gramaldi's heroic survival and Akna's so-called "betrayal" continued to be told by her descendants. They vowed to seek revenge. The disconnection and hurt burned deep into their beings. Gramaldi's greatest fear was that she and her children would be erased from the family tree.

Just as Gramaldi had done, her children taught their children that they had been abandoned, with no one to care about them. She taught them that if they were ever to be released from their icy prison, that they must survive at all cost and by any means necessary. She said that they should also trust only what they could see, explain or control, as that was the only thing that they could count on. Otherwise, it might be best to destroy it in case it may one day want to destroy them.

Aftab continued: "When the long cold cycle was complete, her children's hearts remained cold as they emerged from the mountain caves. Akna's heartbeat continued to pulsate beneath their feet even while they remained so far away. She had hoped that Gramaldi's children would feel the sensation; that they would remember, connect to the whole again, that they would one day come back home. But this life-pulsing vibration beneath their feet was foreign to them. Not only did they not recognize it, they didn't even know it was there. For them Akna was simply inanimate ground that was there only to be walked upon and to serve their needs. By this time, they had no remembrance of the Elixir or the Spirit Eyes. They simply remained closed. They could no longer see any connections between themselves and anything or anyone else. They no longer looked like the rest of Akna's children. They *had become different on the outside and on the inside. It is a sad day when children no longer recognize the heartbeat of their Great Mother, even though that life force continues to pulsate all around and through them; a very sad day, indeed."*

"Meanwhile, over thousands of years," Nokomis added, "Gramaldi's now estranged relatives evolved into various cultural groups and continued to carry forth seeds of The ALL. They were keepers of portions of knowledge and wisdom about this great entity. The seeds they continued to sow over many years yielded secrets of this phenomenal life source and of the vast Universe. These Sacred Secrets deepened and blossomed through the rituals, customs and practices created by inspiration of the Great Spirit. They were given knowledge by Akna of the plants and herbs that would heal sickness and disease. Each group was given a portion and only together would they possess all knowledge and wisdom. They lived in harmony with all living creatures that inhabited Akna. They gave thanks when she sacrificed her creatures for their benefit, both on land and in her great waters. It gave me pleasure to watch as they celebrated the joys and beauty of life beneath my moon glow."

As the siblings continued the story, it became clear that in time, as disconnected as Gramaldi's children had become from their true source, there was something powerful about the Elixir, even as it lay dormant in their veins. Although after so many years, and now in limited supply, it still moved them to unconsciously desire to re-connect with their distant family members. On some level, despite their hatred and denial, they actually did feel a connection to them. In fact, part of their resentment was fueled by an inescapable envy and desire to be gifted with their creativity and even their presence. It was very conflicting indeed.

One day Gramaldi's children found their way home, although they did not readily identify with the others. No longer understanding the nature of these prodigal children, the others who had remained under Akna's love and care, welcomed them home with warmth, sincerity, comfort and love. But Gramaldi's children soon abruptly and brutally tried to insist that everyone live on their terms. It severely disrupted the balance that their estranged relatives had come to enjoy for many years. In fact, their presence disrupted and largely destroyed the entire nature of things.

Shortly after arriving, when they saw how much Akna's other children possessed, and that each group, despite their apparent differences, was relatively happy and at peace, they grew angrier and despised them even more. They couldn't even allow themselves to enjoy the peace, calm and plenty so freely afforded them there. The very contentment of these people who they despised, was fuel for their growing anger. When they saw that cultures and indeed, entire civilizations were built while they were isolated in the caves, their blood boiled. The hatred in their hearts grew. They felt that they had been cheated and were overcome with jealousy and rage. There were beings that were thriving and prospering while they were left abandoned and isolated! They recognized no one and saw no similarity between themselves and the others. These beings looked foreign and strange to them with their dark hue, dark eyes and coily hair. They felt no sense of family with them, empathy or compassion. Instead they passionately waged war against Akna and all her other children, who had no clue that this type of mentality and rage was even possible. So, how could they protect themselves from a force that they didn't recognize, understand nor knew even existed?

Gramaldi's children had emotionally and spiritually divorced themselves from Akna and The ALL. They insisted on seeing themselves as orphans, even though their distant relatives had welcomed them back as family and helped them to start a new beginning. But the story of their abandonment and repeated thoughts and memories of it, provided them justification for behaving with such disdain and disrespect. They saw themselves as being entitled to simply take what they thought they were "owed." A cold callousness continued to rise in their hearts as they vowed revenge for their mother Gramaldi.

With vengeful rage, they pillaged and terrorized as many of Akna's children that they could find. The essence of the souls of Gramaldi's children could no longer guide them, as their Spirit Eyes remained closed – disconnecting them from The ALL. Their spirits were restless and they reveled in creating the greatest living nightmare that Akna's children had ever seen. They enjoyed the cover of the night sky because they remembered the comfort of Nokomis the moon. They felt that she alone had not betrayed them. So, with the moon as their only connection to any semblance of light, under the cover of the night sky was when they felt most powerful. The moon was also the only witness to who they truly were. They showed no mercy. They wanted to annihilate – and many times – and for hundreds of years, and in many places, they did just that.

As they wandered about freely, they took anything they wanted because they thought it was rightfully theirs. They stole or destroyed everything: monuments, artifacts, animals and land. They even stole the customs and histories of their estranged cousins and rewrote them, encouraging all to see life, themselves and others as they did. Although they had now taken control by force, they saw that Akna's children could still connect deeply with Akna and The ALL. So they stole, re-named and re-defined many of their religious practices and rituals and used them to manipulate and dominate them. In doing this, they brought in a lower vibration that then festered into a poisonous virus. Even the once powerful and yet peaceful vibrational frequency of the ground, through which the heartbeat of Akna could still be felt, shifted. It was a weaker, more troubled vibration. And everything affected by this new lower frequency suffered.

Gramaldi's children created systems that were based only on the physical: what could be seen, tasted, touched, and smelt. It was a lower vibration that did not resonate with the heart of Akna; it was designed to destroy her. Many of her other children tried to thrive while following Gramaldi's ways but they could not. Because of the Elixir and the light of the Great Spirit that was alive within them, it was extremely difficult to understand and thrive in Gramaldi's system. Her children believed, for example, that as reparations, they should control all of Akna's resources and make all of her children pay for their use as compensation for their suffering. This would also better ensure that they would be ready when she "decided to wage war on them again." That kind of thinking was foreign to Akna's other children.

They couldn't understand how anyone could think to own gifts from or parts of their mother. They knew that all of these gifts and joys could be "owned" by no one but were meant to be shared.

Gramaldi's children vowed to dominate Akna. They largely used brute force and their analytical and strategic intelligence, lacing all of their elaborate systems with fear. They believed that Akna could not be trusted and would someday betray them "again." They believed that they could only trust each other and those who looked like themselves. This was to ensure that Gramaldi's descendants would remain dominant. The next time that Akna "waged war" on them, they determined that they would be ready. They would have all of the resources they needed and would never be unprepared again. So, they strove to amass great material wealth, land and natural resources. They would be ready for whatever Akna might use to attack. This time they would be ready for her wrath. They spent lifetimes preparing for Akna's "inevitable betrayal" that, as of the telling of this story, never actually came to be.

Gramaldi's descendants wanted to acquire all of Akna's resources. They wanted to take over the water and the land because they felt it was part of their denied birthright. Even though their separation due to Gramaldi's choice to leave and to Akna's internal cycles was extreme, Akna's other children who still had Elixir flowing through them, were also prone to experience the natural cycles of Akna's body through volcano eruptions, earthquakes, and floods. Although they still had the Elixir, and the full use of their Spirt Eyes, the confidence of some of Akna's children in the ability of the Great Mother to supply them with all that was necessary for life, had been diminished as well. So, when Gramaldi's descendants returned, some of those who had remained connected to Akna were also prone to this imposed ideology of separation and dominance.

For others, this form of thinking was shocking and they could not comprehend this radical way of viewing their Great Mother. They could not understand because they had such reverence for her. As their loving mother, there were never any thoughts of possessing her. They accepted that she was not perfect –

as neither were they. But even in her imperfection, they could never fathom hoarding or exploiting the things that Akna had always given so freely.

Gramaldi's descendants moved across Akna with a rage that their distant relatives had never seen nor experienced. Of course, Akna's children would at times fight among each other, as siblings sometimes do; but it was never done with the intention of complete annihilation and genocide. That energy was never introduced until Gramaldi's children emerged from the mountains with the intention of total conquest.

Her descendants violently spread Gramaldi's seeds all across Akna – raping and pillaging. Many times, it was an unconscious effort to access the secrets of Akna's children. They wanted to possess the powerful Elixir, knowing that the secrets were there – but not being aware that it was also still inside them. So, they brutally captured and forced their seeds into the bodies of Akna's children.

"Now," began Akna, "what I am about to say may be difficult to hear and understand; but I have thought long and hard. I have much to say and I hope you will truly listen, see and come to know what I am about to say with your Spirit Eye wide open. Without it, you will not comprehend my words and you may even become enraged." She then proceeded with the following words: "It was a blessing and a seed of salvation for the descendants of Gramaldi to have captured some of my children because they carried the Elixir very strongly within them. Gramaldi's children could not destroy it. What Gramaldi did, in capturing their distant relations, was to try to make them forget who they were. Within many, however, the Elixir flowed so strong that it could not be destroyed. They refused to forget. But many of my children did forget and the sickness took over them. For some, their Spirit Eye closed in sleep as the sickness consumed them. They saw all the power and material wealth that Gramaldi's children had acquired and began to lust after it and in turn admire them. Their Spirit Eyes were closing, and slowly they forgot the power of the Elixir that still flowed inside of them, waiting on the strength and wisdom of their will to be activated again."

"Many of my children fought the sickness of Gramaldi within them. They used the power of the Elixir when they were forced to toil out under the powerful rays of my brother Aftab the Sun, strengthening their connection to me and to The ALL. Many of my children's Spirit Eyes remained wide open, even as Gramaldi's descendants forced their seeds upon them. The Elixir is powerful and the light that emanated from it could never be extinguished. As long as they could feel my heartbeat, the Elixir pumped and flowed throughout their entire beings. They were in constant connection with the Great Spirit and with me."

As many years have passed, there have been many mixings of the seeds. Even those who look like they are pure Gramaldi still have drops of Elixir within them – they just don't know it because it has not been fully activated. And many don't want to know because not only is the Elixir not fully flowing, but the Spirit Eye is still closed. Their hearts have hardened and have turned to power and material gain at any cost, even at the expense of their own future generations."

"For many of Gramaldi's children, the Elixir within them is waking them up. Increasingly more of them are very remorseful for all that their ancestors have done to me and to all of their distant relatives. Some are trying to make recompense, while others are stuck in feelings of shame. They are drawn to the land of AFAR because that is where their ancient mother Gramaldi was originally born. It is where my heartbeat resounds the loudest; it is their root. They want to help. They are trying to remember but they have Gramaldi's seed within them as well, so it makes them incongruent at times in their actions. That is the work that they have to do. The complication is that Gramaldi, in her illness, has spread her sickness all across me and a good portion of my children carry the sickness within them. The influence of her sickness has been deep and wide and has continued to manifest itself generation after generation. My children who never lost their sense of 'home' no matter where they had settled, were unprepared for Gramaldi's descendants return. They had a vibration that was foreign to the rest of my children who did not understand and thus underestimated its influence. This is why my children have to work to keep their Spirit Eyes open and

their vibrations high. If they don't, Gramaldi's seed that is planted within them will take over and destroy them."

The children asked, "Mama Akna, what if we become ill with the sickness that has taken over many of Gramaldi's children?"

"Don't worry," she said. "The Elixir is strong. It will take time to heal Gramaldi's children. It has only been several thousand years. My history is billions and billions of years. So, what you think is a long time is but a moment; and it is too soon to judge the final outcome."

"Gramaldi's sickness, like a virus, spread throughout my children. Even to this day, you can't by just looking at their outer covering tell whether they have built up an immunity to Gramaldi's toxic illness or not. For instance, often, those who look like they should be my children and filled with my light and the love of The ALL, are really full of Gramaldi energy and vise-versa. The only thing you can do is to go by the vibration. Judge by the light force being emitted from them. How much do they seem to resonate with the Great Spirit? What do you feel when you're in their presence? Do you feel a vibrational connection? Is it light? Does it activate the Elixir within you, stimulating the openness of your Spirit Eye or do you sense a heavy vibration that repels? Pay attention. You must. That's what makes it very interesting, to say the very least. You can't just look at the outer covering to know my children's spirits. You can often know, however, through conversations with them. Pay attention to their behavioral patterns. Pay attention to what you feel and trust it."

"There has been much mixture of the two groups," Akna continued, "some voluntary and much by force. The one thing that my children are afraid of is further mixing with Gramaldi's descendants because they don't want their children to become poisoned with the hatred that would separate them from The ALL. And Gramaldi's descendants are afraid of further mixing with my other children because they don't want to be erased, wanting to keep their bloodline as 'pure' as possible. This is in order to maintain the appearance and definition of how they see themselves. With the Elixir still being so strong within Gramaldi's distant relations, her future generations would

likely begin to take on more of the features of those who right now appear so foreign and disdainful to them. They are afraid of disappearing altogether. That is why, even to this day, Gramaldi's children's greatest battle cry is, 'We will not be erased!' They fight for their purity because they are afraid that they will once again be forgotten. Because their Spirit Eyes are not open, they don't understand that even with more blood mixing, they wouldn't disappear. Although they would likely begin to look differently, they would simply evolve back into beings who were once again connected with each other, with me, The ALL, and everything else."

"They are pure evil," said one of Akna's children.

"No," Akna replied. "The light is just buried deep within them and they have forgotten who they are. They have undeniably done evil things but are not pure evil because The ALL is still in them. They are just blind to it; they're sleep-walking and need to wake up. So, just keep shining the light that is within you. They will awaken and remember. Gratefully, many are awakening from their deep, deep sleep. Be patient. It has only been a short while. It feels like a long time because many generations have passed and millions have suffered and continue to do so. But in the time of The ALL, it has been only a very short while. They are waking up. Those Spirit Eyes are beginning to open. Be patient and love."

"They are beginning to recognize my heartbeat when they stand or lay their bodies upon me. Many are beginning to yearn for me and cry out to the Great Spirit. They are learning from many of my children but are having to battle with Gramaldi's energy within them. This energy prompts them to steal and take, to snatch and grab, to violently fight for what they want from others, no matter the cost or consequence. Just like children, they are learning how to live in a different way. They are learning how to share, how to connect without taking from and injuring others. They are learning to love. They are beginning to see themselves more clearly and are allowing their vibrations to be lifted. Their growth feels slow because you are watching them with your physical eyes only; and you want them to suffer for all that they have done and continue to do. When you have that desire, make sure

that it is not Gramaldi's seed within you that is causing you to resent them in the same way. Keep your vibration high and your Spirit Eye open. Leave them to the Great Spirit and all will be well. Trust."

"They have suffered within themselves and continue to suffer in ways that many of them are not even aware of. The systems that they have created have not satisfied their souls. Deep down, they are miserable and angry. They suffer. So, keep your vibration high. The ALL sees and feels your pain. Your ancestors showed you many times how to raise your vibration above the suffering. It is only when you raise your vibration above the clouds that you will be able to understand, know and see as The ALL sees."

"What are we to do, Mama Akna?" the children asked. "How do we heal from such sorrow?"

"The only thing you can do is to allow them to wake up and not allow your own Spirit Eye to close. They are in a very deep slumber. When you are in a deep sleep, how would you like to be awakened?" asked Mama Akna. "Would you like someone to throw ice water in your face? Perhaps, have someone to shake you violently, hitting you while calling you names? Would you prefer to be yelled at and shamed into waking? Or would you rather wake up on your own? Many of my children often like to be gently awakened by the light kisses of my brother Aftab the Sun. The brighter he shines, the harder it is to remain asleep. If you truly want them to wake up, shine brightly my children! Shine bright! They will wake up. They have been sleeping for a very, very long time. You don't have to do anything except shine bright; and be patient as their eyes adjust to your light."

"Help all of my dear children to remember. You help them to remember by shining your light which will help activate the Elixir within them. It is vibrating within all who have it and will allow it to flow. It is vibrating stronger than ever before because it is needed now more than ever before. Many years ago, it was most evident through the physical features of my children. But this time it is also flowing with greater intensity through all of my children's spirits – that will allow it to do so."

35

"Gramaldi taught her children that once they shed their outer covering in death, that it would be the end of them; so, this intensifies their fear of being erased. My other children understand that they are always connected to The ALL and that once they leave their outer covering, they return to The ALL. This is one of the greatest challenges for my children once they have been infected with Gramaldi's sickness: to remember that they are connected to the Great Spirit, all the time. As you continue to shine your lights, it will help to disrupt the sickness and they will remember. One thing that Gramaldi's children grew to hate, was the light of Aftab the Sun. It easily burned them and they found no comfort in it. My other children, however, gained strength through the energy and light of the sun. They preferred its heat, which they enjoyed since their beginning in the land of AFAR to places of colder weather. The only way to bring Gramaldi's children into the light is to help them to awaken the light within them. Help them to remember that they are connected to everything and will always be an important part of the continuum."

"Mama Akna, why are you not bitter and angry? Look at all they have done to you and your other children!"

"I am not angry because they also are my children and I understand. They are at war with me because they believe I waged war against them and my beloved daughter Gramaldi. At times I do become sad, because they are so disconnected from me. I don't agree with their actions, but I do understand. They don't understand that as they try to hurt me, they do more damage to themselves because they don't realize that we are one. I have compassion and empathy for my children that were disconnected for so many years. So, I understand their rage. But it is almost done. They are getting tired of being angry and disconnected; and as they are waking up, they are full of shame and regret. Because the past is so painful, many would rather avoid the necessary healing work of the family and go straight to simply reconnecting with The ALL. They have to learn that the path to the Great Spirit is in 'innerstanding' the oneness in all things. There is healing work that must be done."

Akna continued: "Gramaldi's children are born with seeds of disconnection and many of them grow up angry, resentful and fearing others. Many of them want to rejoin me and the rest of my children, but they just don't know how. Some are beginning to question this and their Spirit Eyes are beginning to open. So keep shining your light and they will continue to awaken. Remember that they too are my children. Don't let their sickness become your sickness. Be the antidote and not more of the poison. Help them to remember and make sure that you don't forget."

"Many prayers have been sent out since Gramaldi's children emerged from my mountains. The prayers are being answered and Beings are coming and are already here with me from all across the Universe. Some have come here to teach Gramaldi's descendants, some are here to assist in the healing of my children who were not isolated in the mountains, and many are here to simply hold the vibration of love high. They are disguised as my children — including Gramaldi's. You won't be able to tell who they are by just looking at them. They are here doing powerful work. Help is no longer, as you say, 'on the way' but in fact, it is already here."

"We are still in the very beginning of the story of my children's awakening. There is so much more of the story that is being written. The healing has already begun and there is much work to do. That is why I am grateful and full of joy. This is one of the greatest love stories of all time that is still being written."

"No man is as wise as Mother Earth. She has witnessed every human day, every human struggle, every human pain, and every human joy. For maladies of both body and spirit, the wise ones of old pointed man to the hills, for man too is of the dust and Mother Earth stands ready to nurture and heal her children."

— Anasazi Foundation, The Seven Paths: Changing
One's Way of Walking in the World

INTRODUCTION

THE GREAT FORGETTING

*Contrast functions as a clarifier. We just have
to decide what we really value. Not from our
heads or hearts, but from our souls.*

Our world is becoming increasingly divisive; communicating with each other across cultures and even lifestyles has become progressively challenging. The ability to build trust and mutual rapport with people from various cultural backgrounds is imperative. How do we accomplish that when there is a continual undercurrent of color-based fear in our society bubbling beneath the surface?

Colorism is a form of racial discrimination based on the color and shade of a person's skin tone, with the preference favoring lighter skin tones. The colorism contrast has resulted in a cross-cultural tension and divide that is impossible to ignore. We have embedded beliefs that have been passed down generationally, all based on the color of our skin. So much energy has been poured into this way of thinking that it is hard to even imagine that there is any other way.

What if we started from a different vantage point? With colorism baked into the very fibers of our cultural tapestries and tightly wrapped around our psyches, is there hope for another alternative? What if we could really understand where we are as a society through this monochromatic black and white perspective and then choose a different value system?

What if we were to distinguish ourselves from one another, not by the color of our skin, but rather the color of our souls?

Achieving that level of transformation would require us to shift our awareness to a higher consciousness, allowing us to see farther than skin deep. It starts with recognizing, acknowledging, and dissecting our sordid past that fuels our tumultuous present. If we can at the very least put all our cards on the table, maybe we can then step into a different dimensional perspective to explore new solutions. By examining what divides us, we can transform our divisions through spanning the spectrum between 'black' and 'white'.

Both 'black' and 'white' are used throughout this book because it is familiar and most of us understand it. While it is inaccurate to many transcultural groups, it is often an accurate depiction of cultural mindsets where the opposition is seen through the lens of racism. They are umbrella terms that ultimately mask our rich and diverse ethnic and cultural heritage.

I suppose if you wanted to create one of the largest chasms and disconnections between two vast groups of people, it would be to call one group black and the other white while continuing to use the standard meanings and defining essences of both words. It is also interesting that black and white are the only colors whose validity is debated. If you were to strictly define them through the lens of physics, neither are technically colors because they do not have specific wavelengths even though they offer the most visual contrasts available to the naked eye.

Black has no hue and absorbs all light. It has long been associated with mystery, power, fear and evil. White includes all colors yet has no shade and has long been used to symbolize purity, goodness, and morality.

Assigning a label to any group – calling one side 'black' and the other 'white' – carves more than just a metaphorical chasm. It divides the issue into 'right' vs. 'wrong,' disconnecting the members of the group by forcing them to one side or the other. Labels that polarize and ignore the space between the two points discount the truth that black and white include and transcend all colors and hues.

"The human family shares a quality that too often prevents us from experiencing the connection we long for; the desire to feel and know we belong." – Lynnclaire Dennis, author

Colorism as a concept came into play over 600 years ago with its seed blossoming into ideologies, systems, and the color identities that govern us today. If the division and power dynamics it has created in our modern society was the original vision and the long-term intention, then it has surely been effective.

As a result, we are finally realizing that we have all been hoodwinked. The hierarchical value system of colorism is not real and it never was. Our cultural differences are definitely real but the manufactured value that we have assessed to one cultural group over others is not.

How can we, in our lifetime, rebalance 600 years of inequity when so many are angry and afraid? How do we do this safely when so many are corded to a power structure run on the energy of hatred, bigotry, and terror? How can we shift a society that is rooted and vested in false values and flawed principles? It seems virtually impossible to begin again from a human perspective. I don't pretend to know all of the answers; however, I do know that we can and must make our voices heard about the direction civilization is moving in. Perhaps 600 years from now our children will look back, whispering through time, thanking us (their ancestors) for being catalysts for positive and loving change – if we indeed do the right thing.

The title of this book is *What Color Is Your Soul?* because I believe that is where we truly have to begin our societal surgery – on a soul level - from the inside out. Not starting at the heart – but going even deeper…to the soul. Similar to how doctors attack a disease by going to the cellular level or the root, we too must tackle our 'racial' differences from a different angle, perspective, and root – a 'soul-ular' root. We must start from the soul and work our way outward. That perspective has to be rooted in the knowledge and acceptance that we are more than the skin that we are in. We are spiritual beings. We are indestructible energy emanating from the same Universal Source.

Many books referencing spirituality or even mention of the soul speak from a specific religious tradition. That is not my objective here. It's been said, *Spirituality is the goal and religion is a path.* My hope is to ignite the fire and draw attention to the goal. Each individual will have to find their own path to stoke their internal fire and keep it burning. Hopefully, it will lead us on a path that helps us remember that we are all interconnected and together we can find a new way to heal our collective wounds.

When we begin at the Soul – devoid of any religious dogma, or as much as we can – it will take us potentially to spaces between our words that we have never explored and new thoughts and ideas we may have never considered. By exploring a different route, our conversations will potentially give birth to new solutions. If we want to experience each other differently we have to first see each other differently. Interestingly enough the most difficult optical illusion to see are the ones that are in black and white.

We are alive at a time when our intentions have the ability to impact mass consciousness in both challenging and inspiring ways. On a human level, our color-oriented conversations have often been filled with discord as well as a resounding agreement that the division it has created must shift. Social strife has always been present, but now more than ever we are hitting a fevered pitch the world over. There is an explosion of information generated around the topics of privilege, discrimination, unconscious bias, prejudice, equity, diversity, and inclusion. This is a global conversation due in large part to the Internet, cable news, and social media where anyone can create a soapbox to present feelings, attitudes, deeply harbored emotions, fears, frustrations, and beliefs. On one hand, this is an exciting beginning because it holds the potential for honest dialogues. On the other hand, it continues to expose how toxic our interactions and beliefs are, especially when vetted through hyper-partisan, colorized, and polarized lenses.

The audience for this book changed over 20 years ago when technology shifted the pace of how we move within a global society. Thankfully our perspectives are evolving in positive ways as we realize how many of our long-held beliefs that were etched in proverbial stone were just flat out wrong. Today, we know our solar system is a speck in a vast universe that defies instruments and imagination. Genetics has exposed the fallacy of the dogmatic belief that the human family is made up of different races. Humans have somewhere between 19,000 – 20,000 genes with only about 100 involved in determining skin color. It is time to look at why, how, and who allowed this tiny percentage to shape self-perception and our opinion of others.

It is challenging to come together to address 'race' because we have always attempted to discuss it from the perspective of 'racism' and the system we have inherited. When we start there it is easy to lay the false foundation that we are different races – unconsciously playing into that false narrative that only further exaggerates our differences. It heightens our fear and mistrust and highlights our painful historic past. We then tackle the problem while in excruciating pain or deep denial.

When spoken the word 'race' divides us. Its vibration moves divisive feelings and attitudes that sets up all manner of chaos and competition. When we stop referring to ethnicities and cultures as different 'races,' we melt the mental barriers that have so long kept us at odds with one another.

Science has presented us with the knowledge we need at precisely the time we need it to understand the inner knowing that underscores our spiritual perspective. Both are essential to address and heal our personal and collective pain. Knowing we are all vibrational beings experiencing the duality of our humanity and spirituality has helped me to sustain a profound sense of inner sanity. This lets me celebrate the richness of relationships, realizing we are so much more than the multi-colored skin suits we get to wear. Beyond a shadow of a doubt there is more to this than we are seeing, reacting, and responding to - and that alone gives me hope.

In terms of color and racism, sometimes it feels like we are in the audience watching a clever sleight of hand game with our attention being drawn and focused on the wrong thing. Is there an unseen practical application to our spiritual growth and development that we are just not seeing? What can we excavate from our painful experiences that will aid in our spiritual growth and development?

What if our time on Earth is a course in the Universe – a spiritual school – and we are all here to learn lessons? As we sort it all out, it would be beneficial to see it from every angle possible. There may be some critical information that we are overlooking.

It has been very difficult for us as a society to walk through the pain of our disconnection.

In many ways, we are stuck in a millennial time loop, running in circles on a track created where we're just the newest generation of runners. The longer and faster we run, the more we realize how small the track is, as we experience our interconnectedness. We are living in times where emotions run so loud that for many it's becoming difficult to sleep or even pretend to sleep. We are individually and collectively waking up. It is challenging not to see and feel when everybody is living out loud with such visceral emotional charge. Even with all of that, we still can't seem to get to the next phase.

Things tend to stagnate because there is an unconscious acceptance of allowing things to 'somehow work themselves out.' This is the nature of racism, bigotry or any such bias. While many are ashamed of its cruel and horrific terror tactics, inaction makes us all complicit in maintaining the status quo. We have to actively heal.

The last thing we need or want is a regurgitation of the collective history we all know. In these pages I offer an examination of the present moment through a spiritual lens and the infinite possibilities afforded to us as we define and create a new narrative. It can happen if we are willing to see one another as equal members of the human family, with the clear intention to heal and grow beyond the past and its pain.

Our wounds run deep and we keep treating them as if
they were surface skin abrasions.

The presence of racism has infected the collective human body like a virus. The fact that it's normalized and permeates every facet of our society means it defies Band-Aids. The longer it is ignored, the worse it becomes. No magic pill will heal it nor will it disappear on its own.

It is time to reframe why we come together and how we dialogue about the nature of human interactions and relationships. The starting point has to be realizing how our biases emerge from systemic attitudes, many of which are unconscious, inherited from our families, school and social circles. Once bias is revealed, the easier it is to shift our attitudes and move towards positive change, mending our relationships and doing some karmic cleanup! This helps us find our way towards common ground, that place on which we can lay a stable foundation to support the vision we build together.

Building a vision, like building a home, requires many diverse competencies. Would you feel safe in a home where the plumber did the electrical wiring? Would you trust the strength of the walls if an interior decorator was responsible for hanging the drywall? In a healthy system, everyone plays a role based on her natural and cultivated talents. Uniqueness is at the heart of a new story, a remembering of the original story where our sameness honors our differences. Doing so elevates respect and increases trust. By remembering our painful past, we can build a healthy future without inducing pain or wading hip deep in denial.

Part One of *"What Color Is Your Soul?"* is titled "The Challenge" because it presents a perspective that is intended to invoke a new way of seeing each other. While it may be an emotional or spiritual challenge, reading it with an open heart eradicates fear and opens the possibility of realizing there is more than one path. Part Two is titled "An Antidote," a potential first step on the path to helping us to remember we are interconnected. Such conscious remembering opens new ways of healing our personal and collective wounds.

This approach may not be for everyone. Some are so attached to their pain or denial that it drowns out everything else. It may seem too simplistic and naïve for some and too esoteric for others. But for those who are ready to look at our colorism through a different prism, then together let's begin.

PART ONE

THE CHALLENGE

CHAPTER ONE

MY PERSONAL WHY

"We've been living the lie so long
that now the lie is living us."
– Lillie Watkins, elder

My intent for this book is to address members of the human family from the perspective of a spiritual being cleverly disguised as a woman in a medium brown colored skin-suit. It is a cosmic dare that asks those who are willing to explore our shared connection through the exploration of our diverse cultural roots. During my 30 years in the field of personal development, I've written two books to support the positive emotional and psycho-social development of African-American girls and women. Key to this was founding a summer camp experience, Camp Butterfly, where we continue to champion their lives through The Butterfly Movement (*www.TheButterflyMovement. com*).

Developing the camp led to intimate interactions with a predominately white population of camping professionals. We worked together on multiple levels from leasing space for my all-girls camp experience, to strategizing with them around conference room tables as a member of the National Board of Directors for the American Camp Association (ACA). I've been a member of the ACA's National Conference Planning Committee, National Board Development Committee, and National Board's Diversity & Inclusion Sub-Committee. As a conference Keynote Speaker, workshop presenter, and training consultant for a variety of camps across the country during their summer staff training sessions, I am now on a path that I didn't intentionally aspire to, yet I have found great satisfaction with.

Over the past 40 years, I have been a student of various spiritual modalities and religious belief systems. It has afforded me tremendous opportunities to study, work with, and learn from a variety of cultures. From indigenous to traditional to New Age, I sought to weave the threads of truth that run seamlessly through them all. The result is a vibrant quilt of consciousness that has shaped, reawakened, and inspired my soul. By experiencing the transformative nature of the 'sacred circles' that connect us all, I have supported both clients and professionals from many cultures in their pursuit of cross-cultural healing and understanding. Forging beautiful friendships across the color lines and industries, I have gained a unique perspective and insight into a reality where diversity is fundamental to unity and inclusion key to cultivating intentional community environments that are cross-culturally agile and nimble. Through my consulting business I take a heart centered approach; focusing on assisting both individuals and organizations to cultivate an increased cultural intelligence, which can be an asset when navigating cultural differences (*www.CrossCulturalAgility.com*).

As the fourth child in a family with seven kids, I grew up in a middle-class neighborhood on the south side of Chicago in the mid-1960s, where even thinking about this path was impossible. My father was a cross-country truck driver who worked hard to ensure that we had everything we needed and some of what we wanted. Dad made enough for my mother to be a stay-at-home mom, and they both sacrificed to make sure their children got the best education, sending all of us to private parochial schools from elementary through high school.

I grew up during a time in Chicago when neighborhoods held strong connections and alliances were deep. The adults in my community and the Missionary Baptist church I attended insulated me in such a way that I had no direct contact with other ethnic groups – except for the white nuns and lay teachers at my schools and the occasional neighborhood store-owner. Even if the storeowner was white, the face of the store was black with its black cashiers and salespeople. All in all, I didn't grow up with 'race' being something that I had to concern myself with on a daily basis. My life was comfortable because my parents trusted me; more importantly, they trusted my surroundings. While they gave me the freedom to explore and nurture my autonomy, the cardinal rule was that I had to be perched on our front porch when the streetlights came on. Roaming, exploring, and playing – just being an untethered kid – led to knowing everyone on my long city block and practically everyone in our neighborhood.

Television provided me with a watered-down narrative about white people and their world. In my mind, we were more alike than not. The plethora of G-rated television shows and sitcoms were entertaining but as it wasn't my daily reality, I didn't know much beyond the roles they played on television. Clueless about First Nations people, the only references I had to them was through old Westerns that played on TV, and the supporting role they played in America's original Thanksgiving story, contrast to the pilgrims' roles as the heroes.

School was another story. The nuns delivered a dull, watered-down version of history that put me to sleep rather than invoked a sense of connection. Like too many educational environments, no one was paying attention to developing awareness or encouraging social activism. Inside my insulated bubble, life was comfortable, fun, and easy. It was only when I got to high school that the sense of carefree slid away and things began to feel emotionally slippery.

I was a sophomore when Alex Haley's movie *Roots* came out, and memories of horror remain from watching all eight episodes. Clueless as to how to process the new and razor-sharp emotions this historical account provoked, a new awareness of my ancestral past felt surreal. This saga, while a mixture of fact and fiction, opened a truth and connected my body, heart, brain, and spirit to many taproot issues that grow out of segmenting the human family based on differences. While the unspoken moral codes and spiritual ethics that governed my community had long been a healthy source of pride and self-worth, the feelings that emerged after watching *Roots* were altogether different. *Roots* tapped into cellular memories that violently ripped away my cloak of innocence and naivety.

Before being initiated into the reality of a black and white world, I thought I could love everybody. There was nothing that my Christian upbringing couldn't handle. After watching *Roots*, I wasn't so sure. I didn't entirely hate white people because, at the time, those who I had limited contact with didn't elicit any emotion. They were neutral, kind of 'beige' – not just in color, but they didn't really evoke any emotion from me. In school, my teachers were kind, probably because I studied hard, followed the rules, and seldom – if ever – did anything to make them focus on me! It's actually kind of sad and accurate to say a big part of me also grew up 'beige,' with an inner and social neutrality that was violently uprooted by *Roots*.

I floundered when my naïve water bubble exploded and I almost drowned in the swell of emotions that flooded my insides. Suddenly seeing the world through new eyes, even my favorite television shows started to help me connect the colorless and colorful dots in society. Watching old Westerns and war stories made me emotionally ill and a spiritual confusion set in as I began to view myself, community, school, and church through a new, grown-up, black-and- white lens. I was numb.

Being a good student led to an unspoken 'given' that I would be the first of my siblings to graduate from college. My parents migrated north from Alabama in the 1950s. My Mom had a high school diploma and Dad had a third grade education. He was forced to leave school after his father was hit and killed by a car while changing a flat tire on a dirt road in rural Alabama. It was later in life that the thought occurred to me that my grandfather's untimely death could very well have been caused by a white man. My father never spoke of it and from that point on, he assumed the role of provider for his mother and two younger brothers. Even though Dad's formal education was short, he was one of the smartest men I've ever met. Full of wisdom, he loved telling stories. He knew something about just about everything and welcomed friends and strangers into his world.

While he seemed fearless, he never hesitated to express strong opinions about anyone, especially white people. As a truck driver, he continuously interacted with many people, but whatever challenges he faced, he kept them away from his children. Dad developed an understanding about people, all kinds of people, and knew how to maneuver around sticky issues, most notably those that involved people he didn't trust.

I remember watching TV as a kid with my family and channel surfing; whenever a black person appeared on the screen, my Dad would make us keep it on that channel and watch whatever show was on. It was only after watching *Roots* that I began to become more mindful of the black and whiteness of this world.

When it was time for me to decide what college to attend, I wasn't prepared financially. Even though I was an "A" student, my 'beige'-minded teachers failed to inform me that academic scholarships were available. Free money for education was most certainly something no one in my family had a clue about. This omission of information is one of the many not-so-subtle ways racism works. The things that are many times automatically available to some are not accessible and available to others.

While driving across the country, at some point Dad decided Michigan State University was the college I'd attend. He lovingly told me that I would become a lawyer and that I was going to make him very proud. In retrospect, I think if he really understood the options I had, he would have chosen a Historically Black College and/or University. I suspect he selected MSU because he believed the world had changed and become available for me in ways that were not the case for him or his generation.

Without question or hesitation, I applied and was admitted to Michigan State University.

Arriving on campus was a stunning experience. I was assigned to be roommates with two white girls who, from the moment we met, treated me as inferior. Not only did they take the same side of any disagreement, but they also made up rules I was expected to adhere to without any input.

It hurts to remember the feeling of living in a room where I was treated like an unwanted visitor. Being a middle child made me a peacemaker and I chose to let many issues slide, instead taking what felt like the moral high ground.

Without a scholarship, my financial aid package meant having an on-campus job, so when I wasn't working, I was usually in the library, hanging out in the student lounge, or in one of my black friend's dorm room. At that time, dorm rooms had landline phones. Since they knew I didn't spend much time in my room, my family and friends back in Chicago would often try to reach me in the evenings.

One night I came back to the room at around 10 p.m. It was a weekday and all three of us had early morning classes the next day. Both my roommates were asleep as I quietly entered the room, but the quiet ended when I viewed the note. Taped to the telephone's receiver was a white piece of notebook paper with the following written in red marker, underlined, and in all caps with several exclamation marks:

"TELL YOUR FAMILY AND FRIENDS TO NOT CALL OUR ROOM AFTER 8:00 PM DURING THE WEEK!!!!"

That was the last straw! I was livid and felt rage emerging from a deep-seated space. It felt like it was rising out of the Earth itself – along with Kunta Kinte, Kizzy, Chicken George, and the entire cast from the movie *Roots*. Something in me awakened that felt equally dangerous and empowering.

While details have faded over the years, I remember flicking on every light in the room and within minutes, the entire population of our floor was at our door, with other students having to keep the three of us apart. Everyone was in shock because this was uncharacteristic of me, in that I had never been in any confrontational situations with anyone. I felt disrespected and unfortunately, I didn't have the self-awareness or the words to express the deep well of emotion I felt, nor the conflict resolution tools that I have now. I was ready to fight and my rage was so consuming that I had no fear. Even though they both were more significant in size, my anger was greater than them both put together. I felt disrespected and was willing to, in the heat of the moment, be expelled from school because of it. They were both about to experience a *"Chi-town beat down!"* I was ready (even though I had never been in a physical fight in my entire life – not even with my siblings)!

Thankfully, my yelling brought the Resident Assistant, who skillfully talked me down before my anger became physical. Being sent home or to jail over a note taped to a phone made it clear I was out of control. Once I was made aware just how high the stakes were, I calmed down enough to understand the situation was temporary. While the pain was real and true, my education was worth infinitely more than the pleasure of settling some score.

Looking back at that night with 20/20 hindsight vision, it's clear my anger was about a lot more than the note on the phone. The build-up that led to me blowing up was a real-time reaction to a painful experience of discrimination and a physical response to the tension seeded in every injustice inflicted on my ancestors. It was a backlash of realizing just how different the worlds my roommates and I grew up in. What shocked me then was how my sheer fury erupted and rose to a Mt. Kilimanjaro level in a split second. At that moment I realized – the hard way – two things: 1) how racism causes a fury of volatile emotions, and 2) how the warm heart and cool head of another human saved my future. It was an opportunity to consciously take a long hard look at what I needed to heal within myself. I realized then that learning to heal myself to the best of my ability was my new responsibility.

Our emotions are powerful and anger, once it is released,
can create emotional drunkenness – causing sometimes
irreparable damage to ourselves and others.

To be fair, the three of us never tried to bridge our differences, racial or social. While cordial at times, they were not inclusive and this made it impossible to find the courage to break down the thick walls that separated us. There was nothing to bring us together, so our differences perpetuated our demise. Like fish that may or may not be aware of the water they swim in, we never found our sameness. We never got beyond our representational selves. Our most common elements, being female, around the same age, attending the same university, and having similar majors, was not enough to find or form a bond, even remotely. We knew absolutely nothing about each other's personal lives.

We remained strangers, co-habiting in our tiny room because the invisible energetic chasm between us seemed too vast for us even to attempt to cross. We couldn't see - and frankly didn't want to see - the invisible connections between us. I don't know if they were ever able to see my perspective, or if they even cared. The incident could have merely solidified their feelings of superiority and justified their further disconnection from what I represented – black people. Both girls chose to spend the remainder of that night somewhere else and the next day when I came back from class, both had moved out. I never saw neither one of them again.

Almost immediately, I was given another opportunity to heal some of my deeply embedded, culturally inflicted racial wounds. The next day, I was excited that I had the entire dorm room to myself! That, however, was short-lived and only lasted a day. My Resident Assistant informed me that I was moving. My new roommate was a sophomore from a small, all-white town in rural Michigan.

When we met, she told me that before coming to Michigan State, she had never met a black person. She only saw blacks in books, magazines, and on television. A part of me thought that my roommate roulette was a cruel conspiracy to get me expelled from school. In truth, this turned out to be one of the most memorable experiences of my life. Her personality was entirely the opposite of my two former roommates. Her spirit was laid back, she was friendly, and never once did she say or do anything to make me feel that she viewed herself as superior to me.

We didn't know our small dorm room was a laboratory where we were discovering one of the main ingredients to successful cross-cultural relations. We compassionately engaged with each other with no need to defend, justify or ignore our authenticity, skin color, and personalities. We began to explore our common ground as members of the human family. We debunked so many invisible biases and were delighted to discover how our similarities far outnumbered our differences. We authentically engaged one another as individuals, painting wonderful memories – pictures that I pull up and from time to time, hang on the figurative walls of my mind.

With my major being psychology and hers philosophy, deep and meaningful dialogues often went well into the wee hours of the morning. We opened our hearts to one another and she became my first white friend. Knowing we were far more than the colors of our skin, we laughed, cried, danced, and sang together, our friendship extending well beyond the walls of our shared room. We opened our circles of friends to one another and our challenges were faced as we made time and space to support each other.

While we were initially an 'assignment', a social task in each other's lives, our friendship was the reason we chose to remain roommates for the remainder of my freshman year and friends my entire time at MSU. To my delight, we recently reconnected on Facebook, picking up our collegial friendship almost where we left off.

My personal history isn't unique. Before *Roots*, I felt safe and sheltered in my all-black, skin-suit world. A world that never felt like it was a result of racism because I was relatively protected and comfortable. I could imagine that for many whites, their parallel universe was similar. If their world was utterly white with little to no interactions with any other cultures, and their perceptions were only shaped by what they were taught by their families, communities, churches, schools, what was shown on television, and in books and magazines, then I can understand how ignorance is born, cultivated, and perpetuated. The truth is that we are conditioned by an unfortunate past.

I understand that more than likely, most white children were fed heaping doses of a not only watered down, but false history of other cultures. This only justified their privilege. I could see how the narrative they fed on cultivated fear of other cultures, denial, apathy, feelings of entitlement, and racist thoughts, actions, and deeds. Internalized racism is hard to root out or even see because we each are wearing our own customized virtual reality headsets. It offers us a private viewing of the world that shapes not only what we see, but how we see it, as well as what it means.

Our general historical recounts are often presented differently than the cellular memories that course through our veins. Many times we are left to react to the results of our colorful histories rather than respond to the causes. These collective histories have the power to trigger our emotions and thinking given how they compound our personal experience and awareness. Their complex plot can terrify and stop us, or inspire and motivate us.

Our collective history makes it difficult to find and sustain our connections, especially interactions in which we lead in with color. It is the very first picture we see, the first impression we feel that subconsciously triggers our energetic defense systems and activates our massive, yet invisible and impenetrable internal walls we falsely believe protect us.

WHAT COLOR IS YOUR SOUL?

*"White supremacy was encoded in the DNA of the
United States, and White people dominate American life
and its institutions to this day, and yet whiteness too often
remains invisible, unmarked, and unnamed."*
– John Biewen, host and producer
of Scene on Radio podcast

When relationships are based on a mutual understanding of why and how diversity is essential to unity, equality is redefined, thus creating fair rules that are naturally equitable for everyone. Without this, racism, classism, and colorism are impossible to dismantle because it is rooted in an invisible belief system, dogma, and ideas that have long shaped our social institutions.

My Dad had an equitable understanding of money and would tell us as children, "If you see a penny on the ground you pick it up because that's money. Respect all money. Pennies make nickels, nickels make dimes, dimes make quarters, quarters make dollars, and dollars make hundred dollars." This is an equitable perspective that many overlook, giving more value to a dollar over a penny. For some, that shiny copper penny has little to no value; and if we believe that, it allows us to walk past a penny when we see it on the ground. Often, we tell people to "keep the change" if it is mostly pennies because we don't really want to be bothered with them. For many, pennies are a nuisance, something to get rid of because we have collectively decided that they are of little to no real value by themselves. Too often people, like money, are not valued equitably. Their opinions, experiences, ideas, and mere presence are weighted according to a false valuing. For instance, the homeless and mentally and physically challenged individuals are rendered invisible to some. Classism is real and can be felt across the color lines with the human value scales weighted heavily against the poor with darker hued skin-suits.

These ideologies leech on to all aspects of our social interactions and fuel the color-coded human value quotient. Partisanship of any ilk requires a wholehearted belief that someone is right and someone is wrong. It requires a serious mental investment that things and people are 'different' when the truth is that there are only differences. It takes courage to be open to explore our cultural illnesses and then find antidotes to heal the stories we tell ourselves that keep us sick.

Today, the challenging task at hand is understanding how to heal and produce a vaccination. When rules of separation are steeped in time, we forget we are stardust, here for a spiritual adventure in a physical body!

CHAPTER TWO

DON YOUR SPIRITUAL PROTECTIVE GEAR

...Keep your vibration high and your Spirit Eye open...

How do we dismantle an invisible system without harboring resentment, blame, and shame? How did we get here? And spiritually, who are we, really? The possibilities are endless, as we ponder our cultural conundrum.

Suddenly everybody is part of this global conversation – both young and old, rich and poor – all colors, shapes and sizes. Add to that a bevy of books that tackle the subject of our cultural divide and racism through the express lens of politics, sociology, psychology, science, quantum physics, and basic human development. I've even read a few books written by religious leaders that probe for answers. This book will be yet another perspective.

Let's look through the lens of deep compassion for our fellow human/ spiritual beings. Let's look with a perspective that is designed to help us embrace our imperfect humanness as well as our true spiritual selves. There is hope. We have to stop pretending that individually we are only self-contained, separate masses of cells that are being held together because they are oscillating at the same rate. We are also individualized portions of the Universal Soul. Beyond our humanness are spirits that want to RAVE® or feel Respected, Accepted, Valued, and Empowered. Respected because it validates our connection to our Divine Source;

Accepted because it is who we are – a small container of Divine Source energy; Valued because we came here to share our unique expressions; and Empowered as we stand in the capability of who we truly are. We are beginning to remember, but our human lenses are so clouded. In a state of spiritual amnesia, we have hurt and been hurt deeply, with pain drowning out the whispers of our connections. We have to heal.

It is like we are all walking around with sticks of dynamite and hand grenades strapped to our bodies as we maneuver our way through active land mines. One false step cross-culturally and we will either blow up or get blown up, so we are cautious and measured with our words. That is precisely why we have to don our spiritual protective gear, join forces with other like-minded beings, and unpack our truth with intentionality and focus. The vast majority of us truly desire to heal. And the truth is our very survival mandates it.

My family and I relocated to North Carolina a little over 5 years ago. Recently, Hurricane Florence hit the North Carolina coast, leaving in its wake significant life-altering damage. Many of those families are having to sift through rubble and debris to resurrect pieces of their lives that were violently washed away. They need support. The long-term collateral damage to their emotional and physical well-being has yet to be seen. When something like this happens, it is not a respecter of persons - all cultural groups are affected. It is a moment that changed the trajectory of each family it violently touched. However, in the midst of it all, people of all ethnic and cultural backgrounds pulled together. Maybe it was a result of the commonality of the problem, or the magnitude of the hurricane. No matter the cause, the end result was that it brought everyone together in a concerted effort to support one another.

What makes racism a challenge is that everyone isn't affected by the tsunami of racism the same. Everyone's emotional and mental homes aren't completely destroyed, nor is everyone hurting in the same way. And yet, if we assess the damage of racism from a different angle, we will see that we all are indeed affected and infected on a variety of levels.

The spores are in the air and there is collateral damage that has spread far, deep, and wide across generations.

As spiritual beings, we have an opportunity to gather up the pieces of our broken society and like an elaborate puzzle, figure out how we are going to create a new picture. How are we going to fix the devastation left in the wake of hundreds of years of oppression and inequity? How do we heal our collective histories? How do we build a less fractured and divisive future now and for the generations to come? How do we ensure that our lack of clarity and action will not further exacerbate the cross-cultural challenges that our children and their children will inherit from us?

To start, we must put on our spiritual protective gear and get to work. Spirituality transcends all religious dogma and separation as it focuses on love and the intrinsic value of all life. There is invisible connective tissue that binds us together beyond our chosen religious practices and traditions – a belief and investment in the healing of humanity and dependence on an unseen positive Source that lovingly connects us all through our life force energy and our individual and collective breaths. If we cannot see our connections and acknowledge the equilateral value of all human beings, then we don't have a fighting chance. Similar to a physical body, our collective fate is bound together.

We need dual consciousness: human
and spiritual awareness.

In African cosmology and in many indigenous cultures, there is the belief that ancestors return. That belief is affirmed when children are born with an otherworldly knowing or a strong sense of purpose or genius. When we understand life, not just through our human filter, but through our soul's experience, then it creates different questions that get us to different answers. Answers that beseech our souls, regardless of the religious lens we choose to view the world and our experience through.

We can look at this thing called race from any angle. But the truth is, if we genuinely believe that we are eternal beings, then there is so much more to us than meets the eye. Our collective attention is placed on the wrong thing if we are only figuring it out through our humanness. For many of us, this is not our first rodeo. Like it or not, we have probably been in relationship with one another over the course of multiple lifetimes. We are just getting to the point where we have the opportunity to unravel our experience, see what we have created, and then decide how we want to individually and collectively move forward. We get to examine the lies, our evolution, and growth. Many are waking up. There is so much for us to learn and to resolve within our own spirits as to what degree we have participated in and contributed to this current paradigm. The ties that bind us are intertwined and much stronger than we could ever imagine.

> *"All major world religious traditions carry the same message: The message of love, compassion, forgiveness, tolerance, contentment, and self-discipline. So these are the common ground and common practice. On that level, we can build genuine harmony on the basis of mutual respect, mutual learning, mutual admiration."*
> – Dali Lama, spiritual leader

With our collective creativity, open-mindedness, love, and ingenuity, we can transform our world. It will, however, be a challenge if we are not armed in the protective armor of love, anchored in the love of a Divine Source, and supported by a host of unseen helpers, teachers, angels, ancestors, and guides.

We know that there is more to us than meets the eye. We must now start living like it. We have to level up. Let's sift through the rubble, girded in our protective spiritual gear, wrapped securely in love. Racism, isms, and all of the divisive schisms that operate within our society are toxic in nature and are toxic to the mind, body, and soul.

We came here to do this work (especially if you are reading this). If you were drawn to this book, maybe there is a space within you where it resonates. Together, we can seriously probe for answers to the questions: What can we learn from a spiritual standpoint that we do not understand about racism? Is there a spiritual lesson that we haven't been able to clearly see to this point? Is there critical information that we are missing? Stay open. The possibilities are endless.

> *If the world were already perfect – what would there be to do? The world is our collective project.*

CHAPTER THREE

IS IT MALIGNANT?

*We are determining the true soul of our Nation;
either through false narratives, rhetoric, and fear
or connections founded in truth and love.*

I was on an airplane recently and the person sitting next to me was a sales rep for a pharmaceutical company. In the midst of our friendly airplane banter, he said, "You know, we all have cancer. You know that, right?" I said, "No, I didn't know that." He said everyone carries the cells for cancer in their bodies. In this modern day and time, scientists don't know which came first. Was it environmental or a genetic adaptation? The reality is cancer cells are in all of our bodies. They are part of our internal ecological system. In that system, they are moving around like every other cell. We have T-cell blockers that are watching them to ensure that they don't go rogue, congregate, or come together and create colonies somewhere. By keeping our immune systems strong, our T-cells can fight them off if they start to cause any trouble.

For the majority, the cancerous cells of racism lie within our bodies – in some, they just haven't visibly metastasized. We all carry the cells because this country was molded with it. Racism, like cancer, is a gene mutation. It has literally and figuratively gotten into our DNA and cells. There has been so much mixing of our genes that it is impossible to determine someone's internal landscape just by looking at them. Prejudice, discrimination, unconscious bias, and full-blown malignant racism all manifest below our skin's surface.

Just like you can't treat cancer topically, neither can racism be treated that way. We have been attempting to eradicate it from the outside, focusing our attention exclusively on the symptoms. To properly transmute it, we will have to approach it as if it were a cancerous growth taking up vital nutrients, space, and energy inside of our bodies.

Often, critical cancer treatment evades some due to a deep spiral of denial. They suspect that a newly formed lump feels uncomfortably suspicious, but instead of getting it checked out, they choose the path of denial. They don't want to confirm that their deepest fears have actualized. To acknowledge it would activate feelings of responsibility as well as a confirmation of its existence. Some choose to not go to get it checked out, hiding it from even their closest loved ones. They only reveal the truth when the symptoms have become noticeable and impossible to ignore.

Racism, like cancer, is an internal process with no blanket cure. One size does not fit all. We all have different pain points that gnaw at us from the inside out. It is our own private, internal battle with mental and emotional conditioning anchored in by generational strongholds.

If only we could use our physical eyes to see and assess the internal challenges and spiritual turmoil that racism causes. Humanity has spent over 600 years marinating in it, holding us all emotionally and spiritually captive. It has created carnival mirror-like dysfunctional distortions that skew how we see and interact with ourselves as well as with one another. It affects our self-image, our self-esteem, even the value we place on our physical bodies and its characteristics. Even though racism affects each ethnic and cultural group differently, our symptoms still manifest in ways that keep our collective societal vibration low.

Materially, we live in one of the wealthiest nations on the planet, although we are emotionally and spiritually bankrupt. We are invisibly tied together in this web of interdependence, tethered together on a vibrational level as a society. As long as it persists, the malignant cells of racism will continue to eat away at the human body. We have to build our spiritual T-cells (Truth-cells) up because it is virtually impossible to fight racism with a weakened spiritual immune system.

The Seven Warning Signs of Racism:

1. Change in emotional habits *(emotionally constipated – unable to let go. Stuck)*;

2. A pain YOU cannot heal *(resentment, shame, guilt)*;

3. Unusual emotional discharge *(overreacting and being triggered)*;

4. Thickening skin or a strange lump in your throat *(hardened heart, fixed viewpoint)*;

5. Difficulty swallowing what is true for you *(unable to admit errors and acceptance of the truth)*;

6. Noticeable change in the size, color, shape, or thickness of a pain *(growing hatred and intolerance for other cultures)*; and

7. Unexpected loss of connection *(spiritual dehydration)*

It is a rare phenomenon for advanced racism to go into remission on its own. It has to be treated.

> *"The things that tormented me most were*
> *the very things that connected me with all the*
> *people who were alive, or whoever had been alive.*
> *Only if we face these open wounds in ourselves can we*
> *understand them in other people."*
> – James Baldwin, novelist and social activist

The risk factors of racism are well known, but few understand how it impacts our society as a whole:

1. **Family history**. Most of us have an extensive family history of racism. The historical perspectives that we learned and inherited from our families shape how we see the world. These perspectives help define who we view as 'other' as well as the intrinsic value we subconsciously place on our individual cultural group. We learn how to 'be' in the world and how not to 'be'. The majority of our thoughts and actions are a direct response or reaction to our family's influence. Often, our families create traditions that become ingrained and embedded as *'the right way to think,' 'the right way to act'* and *'the right way to be'* because *'we've always done it this way'.* Any deviation from these traditions can feel like a betrayal and an insult to our ancestors, further rooting inflexible thinking and fixed viewpoints.

2. **Poor diet** *(Intellectually, Emotionally, Spiritually)*. We become intellectually malnourished when we don't take the time to educate ourselves beyond the commentaries, news, media, and others that mirror our beliefs and parrot our perspectives. It can anchor in viewpoints that are stuck in the past and trigger volatile adverse reactions that are fear based. When we don't feed both our physical and spiritual body with a well-rounded diet of information and food for our souls, we can easily forget that we are interconnected and interdependent eternal beings comprised of stardust.

3. **Lack of social activity**. It can be easy to say that we love and accept everyone, but our disconnection becomes undeniable when our everyday lives lack demonstrative relationships. One can verbally express an affinity for and acceptance of different cultures, but those words ring empty without meaningful friendships that extend beyond basic cordiality across color lines.

4. **Having a low spiritual T-cell (Truth-cell) count.** In a weakened state, it is difficult to ward off any disease. It is impossible to be a convincing champion for emotional and spiritual wellness when you are sick. When our vibration is low, it becomes difficult to see and act upon solutions. When our Spiritual Truth-cell count is low, we only view life through the narrow scope of our physical eyes and not the truth of our spirits. It becomes difficult to respond in love and with love. When we look at each other, what we see will always depend on which eyes we are using - our human lenses versus our spiritual perspective. When your Truth-cell count is low, the only perspective that is available is your human one. Life closes in on us, and our frame of reference is limited to an ant's viewpoint instead of an eagle's.

5. **Spiritual alcoholism.** This includes but is not limited to: impaired vision with an altered perception; having a limited capacity to see the truth and the undeniable connection to everyone and everything; exhibiting a lack of self-awareness, with mood swings; and going from denial to shame to guilt to anger to aggression – whenever the subject of 'race' is broached. Others have to walk around you carefully because any mention of 'race' can trigger negative emotions and verbal tailspins. Spiritual alcoholism also leads to not relying on or accessing your spiritual abilities and capabilities; acting as if your human aspects are all there is; and forgetting that there is so much more to you than meets the eye.

Because racism, like cancer, is an internal process,
our treatment plans have to be different, intentional,
and specific. We can support each other in our
individual battles against racism, but ultimately
it is up to each individual. It's an inside job.

General Racism Treatments:

1. Change your mental and emotional diets *(What are you ingesting? Are you consuming divisive rhetoric that lowers your internal vibration like junk food does to the physical body or do you feed your mind, heart, and spirit with things that raise your vibration?)*;

2. Detox your mind and emotions;

3. Strengthen your spiritual immune system;

4. Remove racism *(Consciously removing flawed thoughts and behaviors. It is guaranteed to come back if it is not entirely eliminated)*; and

5. Radiation therapy *(infusion of a higher vibration)*.

The good news is that there are steps we can all take to heal. At this moment, we get to consciously decide the fate of this world as never before. We get to choose to either transmute the energy of racism or succumb to it. We get to decide if we believe that the disease of racism has progressed to the point that there is no hope for humanity except to surrender to it, believing that there is no cure. Or, we get to choose to believe that there is a cure and do our internal work to bring wholeness into our being and for the very first time, into our Nation.

CHAPTER FOUR

SPIRITUAL DEMENTIA

*The brain turns/looks backwards if it cannot
vision a positive present and future.*

I believe that one of the worst things that could ever happen to a soul is to suffer from spiritual dementia – forgetting that we are all eternal beings. Our world is filled with people in earth suits of all shapes, colors, ages, and sizes who move around this earth, suffering from spiritual amnesia – unable to get past the past, be present in the here and now, or create a promising future due to severe memory loss. It renders parts of them to be immobilized and shut down.

No group is exempt. Racism has supported this spiritual impairment that affects us all, certainly not in an equilateral way, but rather like a toxin that we have all adapted ourselves to accommodate. We live as if what we see with our physical eyes is all there is. That 'reality' causes forgetfulness and limited social and emotional thinking - thinking that is so impaired, that it interferes with our daily functioning. Bouts of depression, anger, fear, denial, and disempowerment are common; each represents spiritual dementia in full effect.

Signs You May Be Suffering From Spiritual Dementia:

Memory loss, mental decline, mental confusion and making things up. Irritability, personality changes, restlessness, wandering and getting lost (trying to find yourself). Refusal to deal with the world as it is. Hopelessness, helplessness, and anger. Forgetting that you are an eternal being having a limited human experience.

> *We can tap into an infinite pool of unseen resources if*
> *only we would remember, and then avail ourselves to it.*

Almost every religious system has embedded within it a belief in the hereafter in some form or fashion. There are a plethora of theories and even scientific evidence that our lives extend well beyond our mortal existence. No matter what your beliefs are, hopefully we can all agree that there is more to us than meets the eye. We have simply forgotten, and as a result, our judgment is impaired and our vision is cloudy.

We forget that there are infinite streams of consciousness and knowledge that we can access through whatever personalized methodology that works for us. Be it through prayer, meditation, Yoga, Tai Chi, mindfulness, dance, song, poetry, writing, nature walks, art (both making and appreciating), mantras, spiritual readings, scriptures – the methodology isn't important. What matters is that these tools are all designed to help keep our souls spiritually active and to help us remember that our connections extend far beyond our physical bodies. These are tools a person can use to keep their spirit in the driver's seat of their being.

Unfortunately, spiritual memory loss can be passed down generationally. When we become consumed with fear of losing anything (e.g. power, prestige, esteem), as well as feelings of disempowerment, depression, and sadness, we become vulnerable. Anxiety will cause us to make up stories, shifting historical facts to assuage any feelings of guilt, anger or shame. It can keep us stuck in storylines that we apply to every situation – generalizing and marginalizing entire groups of people, forgetting that we are all connected. For instance, very few of us were taught during our formal school years the truth of how this country was founded. The Thanksgiving traditions that we celebrate were born out of a distorted version of history that romanticized the relationship between First Nation people and the settlers. Stories can be made up about marginalized groups especially when their voices have been silenced. Without stories from their vantage point, it is easy to create storylines that minimize the negative effects of their historical trauma.

Spiritual dementia impairs our memory in such a way that we can't even recognize the connection of all things. The greatest fear that is manifesting right now is the fear of a changing/transforming nation.

It is only when you are in deep spiritual pain,
do you cause pain to yourself and to others.

So many are on edge, just looking for reasons to explode. That is what makes our cross-cultural interactions so risky and unpredictable. You never know what will send any encounter in a negative spiral. We know things need to change and yet that transformation many times sits just outside of us personally. Our attention spans are short and we are easily distracted and frustrated. Because we carry the cellular memories of our ancestors, we hold on to their thoughts, beliefs, and behaviors. We have to continually be reminded that the cross-cultural issues that we experience today are often byproducts and remnants of the past.

As our belief system evolves, our behaviors have no choice but to follow. There is no magic wand to wave or a special pill to take. So, what do we do while we wait for the world to remember? Be remorseful and change? What do we do with all of the crap we are left holding while we impatiently wait? It is what we do in the meantime that matters the most.

Whenever we harbor unresolved pain, often it changes into bitterness or depression, making it easy to become jaded and cynical. Pain then robs us of our joy and genuine connections in the present. A path to healing can become more visible when we remember and connect to the higher frequency of our Source – be it through prayer, mindfulness, meditation or various other practices, tools, and techniques.

There is a lot of good that is happening, but if
we are always looking back and treating the past
as if it were the present, it is easy to miss it.

We either believe that there is a Divine Source that created us all or we don't. If we trust in that Divine Source, we also have to accept that there is a spiritual work that may exist just beyond our full conscious awareness and comprehension. In other words, we probably don't have all of the information.

In college, professors typically distribute their course syllabus on the first day of each class, outlining all of the required information that will be covered. On the first day, many times those multi-paged syllabi seem overwhelming, detailing all of the subsequent work that has to be done. It all sounds foreign at the beginning because the students haven't learned it yet. Without fail, the information is always filled in by the end of the course.

Unfortunately, we don't receive a written spiritual syllabus when we are born that details our entire human experience. There are classes that we are in and lessons that we are learning that we aren't fully cognizant of. It is complicated because we carry our own individual soul's memories, the ancestral genetic memories that are in our earth suit bodies, and the collective memories of our cultural group. We start earth school with all of that packed into our proverbial backpacks. Together we are teaching, learning, and demonstrating our lessons, no matter where we are sitting in the class.

In this lifetime I'm wearing a brown colored suit. In the past, I have faint memories of wearing other colorful Earth suits; each time, I learn a different aspect of love. Regardless of your physical costume, we are here to learn, teach, and demonstrate love. Our souls carry imprints of our past lives like passports documenting our journey. Our individual souls know the full story. In our humanness, we just don't remember. I suppose it is designed to keep us focused and grounded in the present.

We are all only small containers of energy that are all finding and making our way home, back to the vibration of our Divine Source.

What you do affects me and what I do affects you. We matter to each other because we are invisibly tied to one another. With all of the inequity and injustice in the world, we must continuously and consistently remember that when we work to heal ourselves first only then can we heal the world. Everything changes as we begin to remember.

Many are beginning to remember that even physical death is an illusion and that there is entirely nothing to fear. We continue on beyond death and while we are here, we are to help one another and the planet. We have spiritual agreements with one another that we don't fully remember and most times, don't remember at all because of our spiritual dementia. Even when we think we are fully 'woke' we are still in a dreamlike state because we are not fully aware of who we are and how we are invisibly intertwined.

The illusion of Death has the power to activate and elevate– if we allow it. It can inspire us to run faster, think bigger, reach higher, hug longer, and love deeper.

CHAPTER FIVE

+ + + + + + +

CULTURAL COLLECTIVE CONSCIOUSNESS

*We have been programmed to differentiate
one group from another and that collective
conditioning creates what we call culture.*

How do we heal without continually picking at the scab? We can look at what has happened through the enslavement, genocide, and the European conquests – but then, what do we do with all that information? A safe space is needed to heal all the ways that our collective history fuels our cross-cultural disconnection. We need to recover not only from what is happening in the present, but what has happened in the past. Our cultural interactions are tricky because our day-to-day interactions are often triggered and fueled by the tremendous weight of generational wounds we have yet to unpack, individually and as a society.

It all goes back to the understanding that we are all pre-wired and invisibly linked. The only separation is that we are in individualized containers - Earth suits. Let me share an analogy. Imagine the ocean and all that it is. Imagine if you were to go to the beach with an empty glass container, fill it with ocean water, and then get in your car and drive back home with the container. Would it still be ocean water even though it is no longer in the ocean? Of course it would be. The ocean is a powerful force of nature. When we look at that tiny, little container of ocean water, it doesn't seem so powerful by itself, but it contains everything that the ocean is, only on an infinitesimally smaller scale.

Everything emits an unseen vibration - every living thing. The vibration from the ocean, of course, resounds with greater magnitude than the ocean water that is in the small container. The point is that both are emitting an unseen frequency on or very close to the same pitch. They are linked invisibly together. If you were to pour what was in the container back into the ocean, there would be no difference. The ocean would absorb the part of itself that was previously separated.

> *"You, your neighbor, and a stranger; a frog and the pond scum it swims in; a flawless diamond and a dirt-encrusted rock are all made of the same stuff. Stardust. What makes everything unique is the specific vibration that informs its form."*
> - Lynnclaire Dennis, author

If we liken our Divine Source to the ocean and each of us are small containers, we can suggest that there really is no separation. Every living thing is comprised of Source energy. Everything. Which means that we are connected to everything. Everything and everyone that we see is a small container of Divine Source energy and is emitting an unseen frequency. Just as a radio picks up and transmits frequencies, we are like that as well. We are linked energetically and many times we aren't consciously aware of it. For instance, have you ever thought of a person you haven't talked to in a while and go to call them and they call you first? Or have you ever heard a song in your head and then turn on the radio and the song is playing? Or you and a friend start singing the same song at the exact same time? Maybe you have a gut feeling about something and then later find out you were right? There are endless examples of our connection to the invisible frequencies that are in and around us. And like a radio, you don't have to be tuned into a station for information to be broadcast.

Our symbolic radio stations are the connections we have with one another. That is why individuals from various parts of the country can have a shared experience that is reflected in the way they express themselves. For instance, Chicagoans share a common vibration, as do Texans, New Yorkers, and so on. Each family, community, city, state, and then country share common traits because of the connections through their invisible energetic networks. Through our invisible networks, we share stories, customs, nuanced language, food, habits, rituals, music, art, and dance – culture. We are networked together, and it creates a Cultural Collective Consciousness.

It is an unspoken collective mindset and shared understanding – an unspoken code and specific way of seeing and moving in the world. Even in that, we are not monolithic in our cultural expression. Because we live in 'mobile homes' - bodies that are not permanently fixed to one location - we move around and get plugged into other networks, sharing our histories and learned information as well as collecting new information from other networks.

Our Cultural Collective Consciousness networks can subconsciously contribute to our cross-cultural strife because we can tap into emotions that are deeply embedded that may not be our own. So much unspoken information is exchanged as well as an implicit understanding of shared experiences. We are continually pouring content into the Collective Consciousness of our cultural groups, sharing experiences. That is why when we hear and see violence perpetrated upon someone from our cultural group, it profoundly affects us. Trauma is compounded and shared because it links up with our ancestral history and experiences that are already part of the frequency. This trauma is felt on some level by everyone who is tuned into that station, frequency, or vibration.

When it comes to racism, lots of anger, rage, fear, frustration, and mistrust have been collected throughout the years and are mixed into our regularly scheduled programming with this information on repeat throughout the day.

It would be great if we controlled all the programming and content that is being broadcast through our Cultural Collective Consciousness networks, but unfortunately, we don't. Like a virus in a computer, racism and fear can infect much of the programming that is broadcast. Our shared programming is a direct reflection of it. The majority of the programming is always in juxtaposition to racism and filtered through painful memories, with visions of slavery, dominance, privilege, anxiety, and denial flashing across the screens in our brains.

> *You can't un-see what you've seen and you*
> *can't un-hear what you've already heard.*

Constantly hearing, seeing, and experiencing references that your life never quite measures up to the 'norm' can be found on many non-white Cultural Consciousness networks, as well as programming that promotes assimilation into the white culture as a measure of normalcy and a benchmark for success. Reruns of injustice, discrimination, and violence played over and over again keep many of us in a fight or flight posture all the time.

Programs infused with self-love and self-acceptance are available; however, the challenge of truly internalizing it is often butted up against having our contributions to the collective society hidden or devalued. References to non-white cultures are often prefaced with qualifiers like 'ethnic,' 'urban,' 'underprivileged,' 'underserved,' 'poor,' 'ghetto,' 'exotic,' 'minority,' and 'inner city.' It is no wonder that collectively, we are subject to higher rates of hypertension, high blood pressure, and diabetes – it's all in the programming.

On the white Cultural Collective Consciousness frequency, programming is skewed as well with flashes of selective historical recollections. When you are tuned in to that vibration, sometimes, many times, you can't even feel the racism because of the benefits it bestows. It is difficult to talk about it because the programming on that station feels…well…normal. There is a quiet almost undetectable soothing hum, like elevator music, playing in the background - old black and white situational comedies that reflect morality and goodness. A beautiful picture with promises of prosperity and a strong sense of patriotism and national pride.

If you are in a white skin suit, and the totality of your viewpoint is garnered from your white Collective Consciousness network, I can sincerely understand why you would ascribe to the notion that the best of times are reflected in the reruns of America's fractured and deeply flawed history. However, on the flip side of the 'good ole days' are deep-seated fears: fears of non-whites, fears of retribution, fears of cultural loss of power and prestige, and so much more.

If each network had commercial advertising, it would feature anger and frustration on the black Collective Consciousness station and fear and deep denial on the white Collective Consciousness station. Each group vibrates on a different frequency like radio stations. One is on an AM radio station while the other emits from an FM station. These very different vibrations will continually be at odds unless both stations agree to a new format, new programming, and more importantly, a new frequency.

Our connections are getting quicker thanks to technology. More information is added at record speed and the avenues through which we receive information is expanding. Our shared experiences are passed down from generation to generation through the normalcy of life. Every cross-cultural encounter is processed through our collective experience. That is why we can be so passionate – because we tap into the collective.

Remember that container of ocean water that I referenced earlier? Well, let's say that small container kept being filled with things that were a lower vibration than the ocean. Let's say you added piles of dirt, trash, and various amounts of debris to that container. The ocean water would still be in there, but the vibration would change for sure. The only way that you could get it back up to the original frequency of the ocean would be to continually pour pure ocean water into the container, allowing it to keep flowing until there was more ocean water than debris.

There is lots of information, statements, judgments, and beliefs that are widely circulated throughout the networks. Comments like, '*Racial harmony won't happen in our lifetime*;' '*White people won't change*;' and '*Black people…*' Any time you speak in plural, you are speaking for your group. You are tapping into the Cultural Collective Consciousness network.

Stereotypes are born from our Cultural Consciousness conditioning. With mere seedlings of truth, we are conditioned to expect people from different cultures to respond and react in the way that corresponds to the shared generalized belief that is in our Cultural Consciousness network. When we don't get to know others, we automatically rely on the information that we have collectively assembled for people who resemble them.

For example, one person or a group of people can have a negative experience with a person from another culture. The judgments and emotionally charged feelings are then broadcast across the invisible network. If it were really newsworthy, it would potentially be spread virally across our social media feeds, television, and Internet news as well. Where it has its most significant impact though is through the invisible network because it links up and is combined with all the incidents that are in our hearts and minds that have similar content. It creates trauma that is compounded, and when we get triggered, ignites long chains of unresolved pain – ours and everyone else's – that is part of the network that we then tap into.

Every culture uses their invisible networks and applies them differently depending on the circumstances. For non-whites, it has transmitted reminders of injustice and prejudice with the backdrop of '*Don't trust white people*' and includes hundreds of years of genetic data. For whites, it is the reminders and reinforcement of thoughts of superiority and entitlement. The point is the network is always broadcasting content that then becomes the basis of our conditioned beliefs.

These networks exist and they are multilayered and invisible. We are always connected to them and it broadcasts even when we are not aware that it is. It is similar to the music that department stores sometimes play in their elevators. It is subtle, constant, and we are typically accessing it subconsciously. It creates a coded language between all those on that frequency, which solidifies understanding and empathy within the group.

Understanding that we all tap into a respective Cultural Collective Consciousness is important. If we can bring mindfulness and awareness into every situation, then maybe we can all begin to see and experience each other differently. We certainly can add some new vibrational content. I do believe there is tremendous value when we tune into our Cultural Collective Consciousness networks. It is the part of us that is designed to protect us – lest we forget. It can definitely put us on the path that keeps the sins of the past at bay. The danger comes when we only see from our respective Cultural Collective Consciousness networks. This myopic view can prevent us from living in the present, seeing the world through a different set of eyes, and creating a different experience. Sometimes we need to tune into a higher frequency station and get the majority of our news from there. Having a different perspective will create different opportunities to connect in authentic ways.

Unless you cultivate your own stories and positive cross-cultural relationships, you will only have an understanding of other cultures that are derived from your Cultural Collective Consciousness network, books, biased news reports, TV, movies, and through negative posts on your social media feeds. We have to pour into our invisible networks new stories, shared positive cross-cultural experiences, understanding, and active kindness. If we truly want to help raise our collective vibrations, we have to raise our individual vibrations, as well as find a balance between our Cultural Collective Consciousness network and the vibrational information that we can garner from a higher frequency/Source.

When we truly understand our unbreakable bond and connection with our Divine Source, we can pour more of that energy into the mix any time we choose. That is why prayer, mindfulness, and meditation are so important. It helps to tune our internal radio dial to a higher frequency yielding us an opportunity to access new information. Remember, energy can never be destroyed only transformed.

When we grow, change, evolve, and connect with someone who has a different mindset, worldview, and experience different from our own, it challenges us to literally think outside the box (the Collective Consciousness Box).

"You are not a drop in the ocean.
You are the entire ocean, in a drop."
– Rumi, poet

CHAPTER SIX

＋＋＋＋＋＋

UNPACKING WHITENESS

*"The very ink with which history is
written is merely fluid prejudice."*
– Mark Twain, author

How can we build trust in a climate of such massive polarization? In an environment where injustice is not some ancient and distant memory but is occurring on a daily basis?

Back in 2008, there were whispers from white people who were circulating the idea that when President Obama was elected, it marked the end of racism as we knew it. There was the resounding 'hope' that the goodwill and cross-cultural civility of that moment in history would bind us together solidly. This notion was especially prevalent on that exciting evening in Chicago when Barack Obama definitively won the presidential election and again on the day he was sworn into office on the Washington Mall. It was a proud moment for our Nation. There were feelings of hope that this was the line in the sand where we would collectively cross over, arms linked together, finally transforming our tumultuous history, bringing life to Dr. Martin Luther King's vision, while singing "*We HAVE Overcome!*"

Well, it didn't quite work out like that. That high vibrating momentum was almost immediately followed by the reality of racism and our color and cultural divide. There were surface changes, like putting a fresh coat of paint on a structurally unsound house. Many white people thought that because of the election of President Obama, we as a nation had somehow tipped the proverbial scale and would all just comfortably move beyond racism. Diversity and Inclusion were added as the main ingredients that would make everyone magically get along and move beyond our past into a utopian unified future.

Unfortunately, as hope and the promise of love rose, so did the level of hatred and fear – sprinting at record speed while spewing discord in the face of the fact that we still live in a very color-coded caste system.

Then Donald Trump, who represents an old, traditional style of racism infused and emboldened by a new generation and the Internet, was elected. There are many whites who believe that the current divisive rhetoric and policies do not represent them and their progressive, inclusive, and non-discriminatory best selves. But there was yet another visible line drawn in the sand. Trump became the self-defining way for many whites to distinguish themselves; there were good white people and then there were Trump supporters. Plain and simple. But, how was the average person going to be able to distinguish between the two? Every Trump supporter didn't show up at his rallies. When we vote in this country, we still cast our vote in private. And, there were many non-white people who publicly and privately had his vote, too. So, some white people decided that there needed to be a way to distinguish between the two groups – the good whites and the evil whites; the racists and the anti-racists.

Following the design of a movement set by a group in Europe that symbolically showed their support for immigrants, the decision was made to adopt the same practice of wearing a safety pin on your shirt or jacket's lapel. It was to demonstrate solidarity, as well as an outward show that those who wore the safety pins didn't believe in the racist, sexist and xenophobic rhetoric and policies of Donald Trump. The safety pin was a way of showing non-white and other marginalized groups that any white person wearing the safety pin was a 'safe' and reliable ally. Even though it was well intended, the Safety Pin Movement quickly fizzled out. Unfortunately, it wasn't received by many non-whites in the same vein in which it was designed. What it represented for many was a bandage placed on life-threatening issues. It wasn't the game changer that was needed. Safety pins worn in mass didn't make us feel any safer, respected, accepted, valued, or empowered.

> *"Prejudices, it is well known, are most difficult*
> *to eradicate from the heart whose soil has never been*
> *loosened or fertilized by education: they grow there,*
> *firm as weeds among stones."*
> – Charlotte Bronte, English novelist and poet

Another challenge is that throughout our history, countless whites have hidden their identities under white hooded robes to perpetrate the most heinous crimes while being cheered on by their communities. There is silent, passive racism, which is only practiced behind closed doors that runs rampant through the white Collective Consciousness network. It is far too easy to turn a blind eye, hide behind and support laws within a system that is and has always been beneficial to the dominant group. Now, many are no longer hiding underneath white hooded robes, their anger and hatred are no longer masked, and the rage is palpable and seemingly unstoppable.

There is a lot to unpack. If we weren't so intertwined, I suppose our figuring it out wouldn't be so critical. But we are, and it is. It can be a bit perplexing when collectively the same dialogues around 'racial' issues are repeated – almost verbatim year after year, decade after decade.

> *Black people can't forget what many white*
> *people don't want to remember.*

Recently I came across a post on social media where someone had taken the time to create a graphically designed mini-poster with the following (in all caps), *"STOP BLAMING THE WHITE PEOPLE. I NEVER OWNED ANY SLAVES. YOU NEVER PICKED ANY COTTON. CASE CLOSED."*

When I read that, it helped me to realize why this cross-cultural disconnection continues to persist. Some of it has to do with how diametrically differently we view the world. Whites, in general, have been taught a narrow and separatist worldview. Almost everything is processed from a linear perspective: *We live and then we die; Survival of the fittest; I think, therefore I am.*

On the other hand, many non-white cultures have a profoundly ingrained cyclical perspective – with everything being cyclical in nature. When I thought about the words on the mini-poster, one of the reasons we can't move our collective dial became crystal clear.

The concept of Ubuntu serves as a spiritual foundation for many African societies. It is a Xhosa word that basically infers that what makes us human is the humanity we show each other. This concept is underscored by basic caring, respect, understanding, and compassion for others. It represents a worldview that sees the connection of humanity as a web of families rather than individuals. We are all related, interdependent, and interconnected. What you do affects me and what I do affects you. The connections run, not linearly, but instead cyclically including all the people who are, who once were, and who will be in the future.

> *I am because you are. You are therefore I am.*
> *I am the hope of my ancestors. I embody their*
> *spirits. They are present in my daily life and*
> *therefore their struggles are my struggles.*

If within your group's Cultural Collective Consciousness network, life is viewed differently, it will invoke a different response. If the thinking is linear and there is no continuum to speak of, there also would not be a continuum of responsibility. Therein lies a part of the disconnect - the mentality that *I didn't personally do it; therefore, I am not personally responsible.* Here we see two very different and competing mindsets: one of competition and the other of community.

I was reminded of that while watching a recent episode of Discovery Channel's *"Naked and Afraid XL."* If you are not familiar with the show, it is an American reality television show where a group of complete strangers are dropped in the middle of some remote wilderness, completely naked and tasked with surviving for up to 40 days. In this particular episode, there were eight (out of 13) survivors attempting to survive in an isolated and densely forested part of Africa - naked. As they fight for their individual and collective survival, you can begin to see how their cultural indoctrination shapes their beliefs and thus their interactions with each other.

With dwindling resources, they decide to divide themselves into two groups: Those who go out each day to hunt and those who stay to tend the fire - fetching water and resting. Over time, each group becomes resentful of the other and begins telling themselves stories about how they are a member of the most important of the two groups and are being taken for granted by the other. And at that moment we can witness how a hierarchic mind works. Not seeing the value of every member, they begin to bicker over which group (the homesteaders or the hunters) contributes the most to their individual and collective survival.

That same mindset is prevalent in our society - a mindset and life philosophy that places one group at a higher value than others. It becomes particularly difficult when the group that has made that determination is also the same group that is in both real and perceived power.

Within the white Cultural Collective Consciousness is the belief of superiority that was backed, supported and sustained by scientists, psychologists, religious leaders, medical doctors, educators, and the government. It is an ingrained and instilled belief that other cultural groups were/are inferior physically and intellectually. (Remember, it was only less than 200 years ago that Africans and their descendants were classified as three-fifths human).

As a child, I remember reading Hans Christian Andersen's short story, *The Emperor's New Clothes*. If you aren't familiar with the story, our good friend Wikipedia sums it up nicely like this:

"A vain emperor who cares about nothing except wearing and displaying clothes hires weavers who promise him they will make him the best suit of clothes. The weavers are conmen who convince the emperor they are using a fine fabric invisible to anyone who is either unfit for his position or hopelessly stupid. The con lies in that the weavers are actually only pretending to manufacture the clothes; they are making make-believe clothes which they mime. Thus, no one, not even the emperor nor his ministers can see the alleged "clothes" but pretend that they can for fear of appearing unfit for their positions, and the emperor does the same. Finally, the weavers report that the suit is finished, they mime dressing him, and the emperor marches in procession before his subjects. The townsfolk uncomfortably go along with the pretense, not wanting to appear unfit for their positions or stupid. Then, a child in the crowd, too young to understand the desirability of keeping up the pretense, blurts out that the emperor is wearing nothing at all and the cry is taken up by others. The emperor realizes the assertion is true but continues the procession."

When I revisited that story, it reminds me of how racism is invisible to many white people. The 'system' was structured in such a way that it weaves a false narrative of innate privilege on white people that becomes this invisible sense of superiority that they are cloaked in.

If I were to rewrite the story for this specific topic, it would go something like this:

"The white elite hire public relations weavers who promise that they will help them to justify their position of power and privilege. The PR weavers are conmen who convince all white people (both rich and poor) that they are by far superior to everyone else and begin to weave fabricated stories and institutional structures that justify and support this false narrative. They place this finely tuned narrative into the Collective Consciousness network and then pretend to weave a cloak of superiority. Structural racism is 'woven'

90

throughout the public and private institutions. The notion of superiority is then presented as invisible only to those who are either unfit for their position or hopelessly stupid. The con lies in that the superiority is not real and was just made up to manufacture a system of power. Thus, the elite tells themselves that they can see the alleged 'superiority' and that it is real, for fear of appearing unfit for their positions, and eventually they convince themselves that it is true. Finally, the deceptive weavers report that the suit is finished, pretending that the entitlement is justifiably real. Many of the white folk (some comfortably and some uncomfortably) go along with the pretense, not wanting to appear unfit for their positions or stupid (especially when they see the benefits). Then, a child in the crowd, too young to understand the desirability of keeping up the pretense, blurts out that all white people (including the elite) are not superior, and that the racist system is bogus, unfair, and a sham. The cry is taken up by others. Some realize the young child's assertion is true but continue the sham and go about their lives as usual."

Many whites understand that they are not superior but continue to perpetuate many of the untruths anyway. Some will even say, "*I don't see color. I treat everyone the same.*" Even in saying that, there are hints of the false narrative that have been masterfully woven into the fabric of our society that many white people genuinely don't see.

> *Having the privilege of not seeing*
> *color is indeed a privilege.*

It is an unspoken privilege that is experienced when a person doesn't see color. Because it speaks to not having to feel, see, or intersect with the pain of those whose color you don't see. It is triggering for some non-whites due to racism and classism. Whites have been conditioned to not see black and other non-white people for generations. Many people, especially non-whites who are in positions of service, move through society treated as if they were invisible: domestic workers, janitors, maids, bathroom attendants, migrant workers, homeless people on the street, etc. Many times, it is a measure of status to not see what is so blatantly obvious to others because it has never been a requirement.

If someone insists that they don't see color, what they do see is gender, ethnicity, skin tone, age, facial expressions, body type, body posture, clothing, height, etc., which create patterns of unconscious bias. Every white person in American is born wrapped in this invisible cloak of cultural entitlement. It is invisible, but the deception is so broad that many think that they are indeed superior and that it is justified. Cultural entitlement is like a clear top coat of polish that you put over your nail polish color. It can be invisible to the eye, but it makes the color applied to the nail stronger. Just like a clear top coat of fingernail polish is difficult to see, entitlement works similarly. Even if you can't see it nor understand how it works, it does still work.

> *"A man's character always takes its hue, more or less,*
> *from the form and color of things about him."*
> – Fredrick Douglass, American orator,
> abolitionist and activist

Some are beginning to see their nakedness, but don't know what to do – because there are so many perks to having the invisible suit of social entitlement and superiority on. It is a natural outfit. Other groups opposing this point of view are considered cultural agitators, jealous and inferior, further perpetuating the con.

I can imagine that it would be challenging for a fish to be fully conscious of water while swimming and living in it. The water just is. Like an invisible cloak of superiority, it just is. It is a part of the fabric of this and many other countries because this mindset was distributed all around the world. Many take it on and create societies with the material of classism and the innate superiority of one group over another, denying the intrinsic equal value of all human/spiritual beings.

In all honesty, it will be tough to get to a place of complete equity, because the superiority myth has been perpetrated for centuries. And it is so ingrained that it will take a lot of pouring in a higher vibration to eradicate it. There is so much resistance, denial, fear, greed, and inequity of material resources. We need to focus on a much broader cultural transformation – a transformation that includes our current value system. And, we can't get to a more profound transformation unless we become utterly transparent in our conversations. Besides, we have to talk about white privilege. Here's a slightly different perspective.

My husband and I made an agreement with our son years ago - the tradition of Family Movie Night once a week. The plan was for Saturday nights, but given that our son is now a teenager with a jammed packed social calendar, we're lucky to have three pairs of eyes on the television once a month.

Each movie night, we take turns picking the movie and this particular time, my son picked *Star Wars: The Force Awakens*. Many times when I'm watching a film during family movie night, I am only half watching it, especially if it's late and I didn't choose it. Similar to Homer from the *The Simpsons*, my mind has been known to wander to something much more interesting…like donuts. But this particular movie intrigued me; maybe because it was advertised to have this new main character who was black. I think subconsciously it took me back to a time when I was a kid and my Dad would make us watch anything that had black people in it – so I dutifully paid attention (even though my mind would occasionally wander).

As I watched somewhat mindlessly, it suddenly, donned on me, "*This is how I can explain White Privilege! This is how to explain White Privilege!*" Of course, I was immediately hushed by my husband and son, but the figurative light bulb was already shining over my head. There is this scene in *The Force Awakens* where the Storm Troopers come and attack the Resistance, which is comprised of a variety of oppressed cultures. The Storm Troopers are in these white suits and they wreak havoc everywhere across the galaxies. They are taking folks' land, killing or capturing other cultures, enforcing all these crazy rules…they are the ultimate bad guys.

In *The Force Awakens*, this one Storm Trooper decides he isn't going to fight for the Galactic Empire anymore and decides that he is going to align himself with the Resistance.

At first, members of the Resistance don't trust him because there has never, in the history of *Star Wars* and particularly the history of the Storm Troopers, been a Storm Trooper to go rogue! They didn't initially trust him. Even though he was fighting with them instead of against them, they still didn't believe him. It was only when he removed his helmet/mask to reveal himself that they began to trust him. He had to reveal to them who he really was on the inside. He then put his helmet/mask back on and continued to fight with them.

The privilege part was that he was able to get them into areas of the Empire that they couldn't get into on their own because they didn't have the Storm Trooper suit on. My point is sometimes privilege can look like that. It is like an All Access Backstage Pass. Using the privilege afforded to him by his white Storm Trooper suit, he was able to get the Resistance into places that they couldn't get into on their own, as well as do things that they couldn't do at all.

If he had thought in his mind and even made just a verbal proclamation that he was fighting with the Resistance but didn't follow it up with any actions, his words would have rang hollow and been meaningless. He had to actively show where his allegiance was.

If you are identified within our society as belonging to the white cultural group, then the external color of your body (which I also refer to as your Earth suit or skin suit) gives you Storm Trooper privileges. You can, however, go rogue and use that privilege in active support of the Resistance. You can use your privilege to get into places that others can't. You can change things in ways that others can't who don't have access. You have privileges that are automatically afforded to you through your Storm Trooper suit, but you also inherit all of the sordid histories that are attached to it as well.

Because of the culture that white people inherit, it is difficult and pretty much impossible, for a white person to see themselves from inside the Storm Trooper suit and through the eyes of non-whites. Sometimes, your good intentions may not be received in the same ways that you intend. Non-whites may only see your white Storm Trooper suit and not your intentions. Assumptions may be made that you are racist and therefore not to be trusted. So, don't be taken aback when other cultures viscerally respond negatively to you. Many will not see a person attempting to help. They will see you as a white Storm Trooper. Similar to *Star Wars*, our collective history is an epic tale that spans many generations. Your skin suit most likely will trigger different responses from different people based on their personal and historical interactions with people who look similar to you.

Unless you open your heart and authentically demonstrate who you are, assumptions may be made that you are a regular Storm Trooper. You become an adverse representation simply because of the skin-suit you inherited.

It may not seem fair, but the only way that other cultures will know and trust you is by you taking off some of your protective gear (which is also true in any relationship). And, it would be good to check and make sure that the vibration that is emanating from your individual suit is of a high frequency. In other words, make sure that you are not vibrating fear and superiority. The only way that others will know who you really are is when you reveal your heart through your actions.

There is absolutely nothing wrong with admitting that one has white privilege; that alone does not mean that you are a racist. Rather, it says that you recognize that you inherited a legacy of systemic privilege and systemic oppression that disadvantages non-white people. It is not only about how you perceive yourself. It is about how others view you as well – especially if the desired outcome is authentic connections and actionable ally-ship.

Just like if we were at a costume party, your costume would evoke stories that stem from other party goers' memories and experiences – both personal as well as those that are in the Collective Consciousness. How do you transcend the skinsuit? How can you help us to see you beyond the costume? You do this by becoming different than the perceived character. Show yourself to be more than just your skinsuit. Transcend it. Be a consistent and trustworthy demonstration of evolved consciousness.

You have a tremendous opportunity to effect change in the system/empire. For instance, when you are in private meetings with others who wear the Storm Trooper suit, you can advocate for equity and reparations for other cultural groups; you can help change policies and laws; you can stand up in the face of bigotry, hatred, and injustice, etc. You can be brave and open yourself up to other cultural groups, cultivating authentic heart-to-heart and soul-to-soul interactions and friendships. I believe there are many rogue spiritual beings in Storm Trooper suits out there. It is your responsibility to educate yourself and see where racism resides within you – whether it is on the surface, just below the surface, or deeply embedded.

Today, most initiatives of inclusivity and diversity are not messages for non-white populations. They are for white people. I can almost guarantee that most non-white cultural groups are not sitting around pondering how to 'include' white people. It is a one-sided conversation that white people are having and mostly they have it with other white people. That is the challenge. Typically, there is not the diversity of ideas, perspectives, and physical bodies present in the room to solve the problem of diversity and inclusion. Often, the challenge of addressing the lack of diversity is tasked to a non-diverse group of white people spinning ideas amongst each other, and many times, that is how things go awry. Marketing and corporate executives, movie producers, government officials, and others get it wrong by super-imposing a stereotypical understanding onto cultural groups that are not in positions of power and influence, nor are they in the room or at the table when critical decisions that directly affect them are made.

During this societal shift, we need all hands on deck. We need every rogue white person to consider the privilege that your skinsuit affords you and then show up unapologetically ready to stand <u>with</u> the Resistance, understanding that you can't lead the non-white Resistance.

You must be comfortable doing what is right, not for the accolades and high fives from non-whites, but rather, doing what is needed and morally imperative – even when no one is watching - because it is the right thing to do. Any time you do something that positively contributes to bringing us collectively into balance, it shifts your energy and others will notice. The consistency of your actions builds trust beyond any words you may say.

The only time you need to feel bad about your privilege is if you are using your privilege to make others feel bad.

The irony of all ironies is that in the movie, the rogue Storm Trooper was really a black man deep on the inside. It was buried under a seemingly impenetrable white exterior. Our human connections trace us all back to our ancient ancestors on the continent of Africa, and our spiritual connections trace us back to our one Divine Source. It is the histories and cellular memories that are encoded in the Earth suits that keep us disconnected on so many levels. To heal, we have to peel back our protective layers to remember who we really are.

Our depth of love is demonstrated and known when love is threatened and we stand up for it.

What are you doing with your All Access Pass? Have you actively joined the rest of the family and the Resistance? Use your powers for good.

CHAPTER SEVEN

✦✦✦✦✦

THE NORMALIZATION
OF VIOLENCE

You never die from a snake bite. The bite itself
doesn't kill you – it is the venom that kills you as it
poisons the system long after the bite has occurred.

Violence. Defined as using physical, emotional and psychological force to injure, abuse, damage or destroy. It sits at the very heart of our collective experience in this country. It becomes a tricky subject because many of us have seen and experienced so much violence until it is normalized in ways that we no longer even recognize. Violence should be traumatic when we look at it, but because we were born into a society that was founded violently, it lives in us in ways that we can't see, recognize, nor many times directly feel. We are becoming more and more desensitized to it. It is a slow, constant drip.

There are numerous examples where we experience it and then move on. We witness it, then move on. We get angry, then move on. We applaud it if we believe it is justified, then move on. It's normalized and accepted. We speak violence to each other even in our daily interactions. Have you ever said or heard any of the following: *I could kill you. If looks could kill. That kills me. She/he slays. Bring out the big guns. Twist your arm. Under the gun. Ride shotgun. Killing me softly. Breaks my heart. At the end of my rope. Bite the bullet. Roll with the punches. Get away with murder. Overkill. Killer smile. Soften the blow. Kill two birds with one stone. Shot in the dark. Pushover. When push comes to shove. Shooting off at the mouth. Take a shot at it. Shooting the breeze. Locked and loaded. Beats me. Break a leg. Need more ammunition. Moving target. Bang for your buck. Take a stab at it.*

How do we connect when we have a plethora of opportunities to witness, identify with, and incorporate violence? Well, we learn a lot from the media. Many dramas and movies mix reality with fiction, making our database of violence robust. Our favorite actors play out real-life themes on the screen. Nowadays, even news pundits are hired to play themselves in both television dramas and movies. Fusing reality with fantasy and fiction, connects us more intimately with the storyline. Our brains process the imagined as real. The result is that often we imitate what we see and hear, subconsciously mirroring the behavior or at the very least it goes into our database of possibilities and probabilities. We emulate what we see, giving us behavioral options if we're ever faced with similar circumstances.

I fondly remember one of my favorite childhood rituals was to wake up early on Saturday mornings, while my parents slept, pour myself a bowl of cereal and milk and sit in front of the family television and watch cartoons. I watched *Bugs Bunny and Daffy Duck, Tom and Jerry, Casper the Friendly Ghost, Roadrunner, and Wylie Coyote, Sylvester and Tweety Bird, Mr. Magoo, the Jetsons,* and *Flintstones,* just to name a few. I would spend the morning watching hours of cartoons. As I look back, many of those cartoons were extremely violent, with the undercurrent of sexism and racism. Bodily harm and dismemberment were commonly played for laughs. The characters would do things that would typically severely maim or kill a person, and then in the next scene, they were back again, magically regenerated and completely unharmed.

It wasn't just cartoons; violence was played out in many seemingly innocent 'family-friendly' shows. As kids, my siblings and I would watch the *Three Stooges*, for example, until our Dad put a stop to it, forbidding us from watching it. We thought that it was just another harmless and laughable physical comedy like *I Love Lucy* or one of the many *Jerry Lewis* movies.

However, there was something about the *Three Stooges* that rubbed my Dad the wrong way. He said after watching the *Stooges* we would become them, and in fact, we did! I remember him saying, *"I'm not raising stooges! Turn that mess off!"* I definitely can understand now. Long after watching their antics, we would mimic Curly's backward shuffle and his *"Woop-oop-oop-oop-oop-oop!"*, *"Nyuk, Nyuk, Nyuk,"* *"Oh, a wise guy, eh?"* and *"Soitenly!"* (certainly). We would imitate Moe's catchphrase: *"Why I oughta…"* and his slapstick antics like slapping his fist down so it could wind in a circle and bonk one of the other stooges on the head or making a 'v' with two fingers in an attempt to poke their eyes out. We would playfully mimic their moves with such precision it is a miracle we didn't maim or seriously injure one another!

We live in a culture of violence that is normalized in such a way that even in movies, the actors who portray characters that perpetrate horrific acts of violence are understood and sympathized with. They become heroes that are immortalized and admired for their strength, cunning, and courage. An example of this includes iconic movies like *The Godfather, American Gangster, John Dillinger, Scar Face, Bonnie & Clyde, Dog Day Afternoon, Good Fellas, The Wolf of Wall Street, Chopper, Pulp Fiction,* and *Training Day*, to just name a few. Emphasis is always placed on the 'justifiable' violent acts with less attention - if any- on the emotional collateral damage in the hearts and minds of the loved ones who are left behind. That aspect is usually only portrayed in the face of some sort of retribution theme in the movie. There is a callous disconnection to the aftermath of violence that models a lack of emotional accountability and empathy for the victims and their loved ones. As viewers, we unconsciously make that disconnection as well.

We accept violence as a way of life. It can be both horrific and addictive. The dualistic fight – that is how it is justified. Good versus Evil. Right versus Wrong. It is the ultimate battle that seeps into our interactions, our language, and media. The irony is that in any struggle, argument, disagreement or war, both sides think they are right and justified.

To further complicate things, we carry the historical remnants of our ancestral battles and the threads of cellular memories, with the ever-present reminders of injustice, prejudice, and privilege - both denied and inherited. It gives us constant reminders of why we should continue to be angry, divided, and afraid. And boy, is our database of violence robust! We are triggered daily – each time we witness violence against others in our cultural group. I can only imagine the cellular damage or epigenetic gene variation that has occurred in our bloodlines due to the perpetuation and witnessing of extreme acts of violence towards other human beings, as well as human semblances (realistic video game avatars and cartoons). As humans, the pathology is in us all. Nobody gets a pass. We all carry the seeds of violence within us.

As a species, we are currently caught up in the 'otherness' and pain that we can't even see solutions without violence – violent words, anger, and rage. We are in a dysfunctional relationship cross-culturally. It is just like a family whose members are violent with each other. The children grow up perpetrating violence either on others or mainly onto themselves and within themselves. Unfortunately, we all have a common dysfunctional family background. My ancestors came here in dysfunction. This country was founded with violence and dysfunction. What happened to our Indigenous American and African ancestors in this country was horrifically violent and unspeakably dysfunctional with the remembrance of it being passed down generationally with the compounded trauma still present today. While we are all interconnected, the foundation of this country is divisive and hateful in nature, bolstering a false sense of superiority, selfish agendas with a lack of compassion and empathy for the 'others'.

Separation has to happen to perpetrate violence. That separation is what has been passed down. It is a pathology that founded this country. It continues to be spread and is unchecked because it is seen as normal –

the pathology of hatred for anyone who challenges that position. Many non-whites carry trauma that is not post-traumatic, but rather, Still In Trauma Experience (S.I.T.E.), compounded generationally. For many whites, it shows up as disconnection, denial, and an exaggerated patriotic defensiveness, or stated simply, defending the decisions, actions, and traditions created by their ancestors.

Throughout history, the 'other' mentality had to be accepted to perpetrate violence. It is not normal to perform violence on our own bodies. Violence, once it seeps into our psyches, lowers our vibrations. If we can't retaliate, the loss, grief, hopelessness, despair, and lack of forgiveness can cause us to implode.

The idealized version of who we think we are as Americans make it difficult for us to see who we really are. Until we are willing to look at and own our cultural addiction to violence, lasting peace and equity will always be a distant fantasy. How can we gain peace and equity while consuming violence? It is difficult because it renders us incongruent.

The real battle is the battle of Light and Darkness within each of us. It is our individual and collective human psyche damage that is most disturbing. If this is who we are, then we may as well accept it, and battle until the physical death of us all. Or we can realize as spiritual beings that from the beginning, it was never a good idea to start a nation with violence as the foundation. This is the result. The damage doesn't have to be permanent, but it will take a lot to shift it because we are so addicted to it.

Imagine if the Earth was a physical person with all of the characteristics of a human being: eyes, nose, liver, spleen, heart, legs, etc., with all of the internal organs and systems working together to support the well-being of the whole. In a healthy body, the heart doesn't attack the liver. The kidneys don't fight against the gallbladder. If one part of the body dies, it could mean death to the whole body. They seamlessly would work together for the preservation of the whole.

I judge that, if our planet were under attack by aliens, we would band together to protect it. We've already seen that theme played out in blockbuster movies: the Earthlings versus the Aliens. If there were some outside threat, like an alien invasion, then the color of our Earth suits wouldn't matter. As citizens of this planet, we would work together just as any '*body*' would.

When we consume violence, it disconnects us from aspects of the rest of the human body and the truth of who we are. If under normal circumstances, it is difficult to inflict mortal pain onto ourselves, then we would have to create a disconnection to inflict violence onto someone else. Somewhere within our hearts and minds, we have to disconnect and shut down our emotions enough to create some type of separation. A '*me*' versus '*you.*' An '*us*' versus '*them.*' We have to create separation. Unless something is chemically wrong or imbalanced in our brains, it is challenging to inflict mortal pain to ourselves. Typically, the assistance of some sort is necessary. Something or someone will have to play a role. For instance, just on your own, the average person can't hold their breath until they die. You would need the assistance of some other object or person. Our default setting wants to be here. We want to live and not die. We fight for our lives. If we could realize our connections, we would value the lives of everyone.

There are so many things to be angry about in the world; the danger comes when low vibrating frequencies outside of us team up with low vibrating frequencies within us. In other words, the problem is when the external violence that is presented to us in the world connects with our internal violence. It makes us defensive, explosively angry, callous, fearful, depressed, disconnected and aloof. The broader question is: *When we speak violence to each other, is it originating in the present or is it an echo from voices in the past?*

Violence and our consumption of it – both knowingly and unknowingly, consciously and subconsciously – is essential because violence is a different vibration than love. When we are connecting to violence either internally or externally, it lowers our vibration. When we link to it, we can't get to love, we can't get to peace. We normalize it as a way of being. Whenever we are in a conflict, violence is a viable option. It starts with how we talk within and to ourselves, and that is reflected in how we engage with one another.

People who are emotionally and spiritually grounded, peaceful and loving, are less likely to be violent towards themselves and others. Our challenge is to raise our vibration high enough so that we can access other solutions. Our challenge is to rise to spaces of love – not tolerance, but equanimity and a true desire to want the best for everyone. The reason that it is hard to wish the best for everyone is that we have elephant-like memories and we don't see the connections between us.

Many years ago I was a flight attendant, and every year we would have to participate in mandatory safety drills. We would go through simulations of every in-flight crisis imaginable. One of the several different protocols for dealing with a potential hijacker was to try to make eye contact. Try to help the hijacker to see you as a fellow human being and not a threat. If the circumstances were right, we were instructed to talk about our children, our families, our desire to live and why, all while making eye contact. The hope was that by making eye-to-eye contact, it would lead to a soul-to-soul connection and the hijacker would soften, and hopefully, he would remember our human relationship and have mercy.

I'm grateful that I was never put into a situation where I had to use this tactic 30,000 feet above the ground. I do know from experience that many times when I have been in the face of anger that is directed towards me, if I meet that aggression with a vibration that is higher in frequency, it helps to diffuse it.

When our frequency is high, we vibrate higher. In the words of our former First Lady Michelle Obama, *"When they go low, we go high."* In essence, we have to raise our vibration. We can't solve problems at the same frequency that they originate. The old adage of 'fighting fire with fire' never works. Firemen don't walk around with fire to put out fires. It doesn't make sense. That is why we can't get to peace through war. They are two different vibrational frequencies and the gap between them is vast.

Our challenge as a society is to rid ourselves of the notion of a hierarchy of Human Value, which in essence implies that one individual, group or culture is worth more or less. If we can pull our visual perspective out even further, we will not only see our connection to all of Hue-man-ity, we would also see our link to the planet itself and everything on and in it.

If we genuinely want peace and to live in a world that honors life, then we have to become more conscious and aware of what we are feeding on - the things that we are consuming. Find the balance and then live in contrast. Contrast is different than violence; it is evidence of growth. For example, light is only relevant in contrast to darkness. Contrast functions as a clarifier; sometimes the clarity of what we want is only realized in the depths of experiencing what we don't want. We just have to decide what we really value – not from our heads or hearts, but from our souls. Do we want more of the same or are we ready to try something different? Just as smoke rises out of the ashes, we can grow to a different worldview. The higher we go, the better we can see the connection to everything.

My prayer is that we no longer sit in the space of unawareness and how it affects us. On a spiritual level, we know that we are eternal beings, but it is our humanness that continually lowers our vibrations. It is one of many vital barriers that prevent us from getting to societal peace and love. Even for me I have had to shift my awareness. I have never been able to watch horror movies and would much rather watch a good comedy than a horror flick with laughter prevailing over fear any day! I made a conscious decision to eliminate horror movies from my diet completely. There is definitely, however, a market for the macabre. It seems that violence is acceptable only on our terms though as long as it is on the big screen. When it leeches into our personal reality, it seems that it is no longer overlooked. I certainly don't want to get into a debate over gun control and violence because that would lead down an entirely different path triggering a stuck point for many.

Part of the challenge is that underneath the skin layer, many of us are angry and disconnected and very protective and defensive about our pain. Our collective vibration is so far removed from where we would like to go and the idealized version of who we want to be as a society. We are in desperate need of transformation. We need an infusion of new and uplifting content into our collective societal consciousness. If we can at the very least, be willing to shift our perspective, it would in turn, shift our vibration and we would get to love.

Love. As it continues to show itself,
are we too angry and afraid to notice?

Love is the most potent force in the universe (or at least on this planet), and because of its power, we are many times afraid of it; afraid to show love, to embrace love, to be loved. Often, we see love's power and become worried. Worried that it will render us blind, vulnerable and weak. It becomes both what we desire and fear at the same time. So we tend to approach our cross-cultural tensions from a perspective that appears to be more comfortable and many times stronger – fear. Fear is many times much more accessible and easier to express because we have developed walls around our hearts to protect our love.

On the Internet, stories that are negative, violent, and racially charged are always given airtime and are spread throughout social media like a wildfire. We are definitely pouring more negative stories in – more often than not. When someone does something negative or violent, it is poured into the collective consciousness and it goes viral. We just have to be aware and make it a point to pour in more good – making that goodness go viral. Similar to the earlier "ocean in the container" analogy, we just have to pour in more good by flooding the collective consciousness with positive stories to shift the vibration so that it becomes a cultural reality.

PART TWO

AN ANTIDOTE

CHAPTER EIGHT

♦ ♦ ♦ ♦ ♦

ALL MY RELATIONS:
HEALING OUR ANCESTRAL ROOTS

*Current science and anthropology believe that all
humans come from Africa. A large number of black
people in America have white ancestry. Many black
and white people have red ancestry. Many red
people have black and white ancestry. If we truly
care about future generations, we have to heal. We
are the cracks all of our children fall between.*

I f we could see with our spiritual eyes how much we are loved and
who surrounds us every minute of every day, we would experience
far less loneliness, depression, and disconnection.

What a tremendous gift it is to have a physical body during this
incredible time in our journey together! Each of us is individualized yet
invisibly connected. If we could only see ourselves and others the way
we indeed are — beyond our costumes, masks, and coverings — what a
blessing and shift in conscious awareness that would be.

*If we could see with our physical eyes the
threads that bind us to each other, undoubtedly
it would disarm all hostility.*

It is only natural that we wonder about our roots, wanting to know who we are and why we are. This curiosity anchors us in the human family tree. There is an almost indescribable feeling when you know your family origins. We take great pride when the lineage is strong and admirable. For instance, if I were a known blood descendant of Harriet Tubman, I would have more than likely mentioned it in the first few pages of this book. The thought of being connected to her tenacity, courage, and strength, would give me an extra pep in my step. A boost to my esteem. To know beyond a shadow of a doubt that she was a part of the fibers that knitted me together in my mother's womb would embolden and strengthen me. I would consciously draw on her strength when needed.

As science and technology evolves, the scientific breakthroughs in our understanding of DNA and epigenetics also have advanced. We can trace back our ancestry for hundreds of years. For many of African descent (myself included), we thought that information was long gone. Many have tried to reconnect the fractured and disassembled branches to our family trees that were ripped away through the enslavement of our African ancestors. We all want to know who we are and our real roots. For me, it has always felt like we were cheated out of our history. Like plucked flowers from a garden, stems cut, then placed in a variety of vases around the world, our longevity was limited since we were no longer connected to our specific genetic roots.

When the movie *Black Panther* was released, it was monumental and provided a significant boost to the Collective Consciousness of black people. The film offered a different perspective than the slave narratives that are often presented when our history is shared on the big screen. Our on-screen story many times begins either with our African ancestors capture and enslavement, the slave ships, or after we arrived in America on southern plantations. There was little to nothing available in the mainstream about who we were before this violent disruption. From a human perspective, it has left a void. Before companies like African Ancestry (*www.AfricanAncestry.com*), very few of us were blessed to be able to trace our family lines back to Africa beyond just a general over-arching region.

I was glad to replace visions of Alex Haley's movie *Roots* with visions of Wakanda and the movie *Black Panther*. Even though the film was fictitious, it hit many of us in the gut. We celebrated Wakanda as if we were all descendants of this newly discovered place that was hidden and untouched by colonizers. It was the first time that we could see African excellence expressed across the board because truthfully, Africa's excellence has always – for the most part – remained a mystery. We planted the movie deep within our collective consciousness, breathing in the story and the colorfully vibrant visual tapestry of *'home.'* It was a faint memory of a familiar and distant place that resonated deep within us. We could all imagine a time and space that was untouched and where we, like flowers, could root and grow unencumbered and undisturbed.

The older I become, each time I look in the mirror, more and more of my mother's face magically appears. When I look at my son, I see pieces of my face fused with parts of my husband's. He has my eyes and my husband's round face, both of our sensitivity and creativity, my Dad's sense of humor and an analytical mind like my Father-in-law; the list goes on and on. Very little of his personality is an entirely unique injection because he has within him many manifested ancestral seeds that have blossomed. When my son repeats phrases that my Dad would typically say, even though he was less than a year old when my Dad transitioned to the spirit realm, I smile. I know beyond a shadow of a doubt that the continuum is real.

I find it fascinating when I hear stories told by my mother of my grandmother. In listening, I can see parts of my personality through our shared likes and dislikes. Each generation mixes the genetic materials of two distant families to create new beings on the planet. Mixing the family seeds to make us believe that our thoughts, likes, dislikes, personalities, gifts, and temperaments are unique and ours alone.

As an adult, I have had to do my share of personal development work to root out of my personality dysfunctional behaviors that were passed down to me as a child. For instance, my parents solved problems (especially with each other) through verbally volatile arguments or by giving each other the silent treatment. Usually, when my Dad had one too many beers, it would loosen his tongue and he would verbally lash out at my Mom. She would meet his frustration with her own passionate rebuttals. They would yell and argue with neither of them listening to the other. Once the argument ended, it was always followed by a deafening silence between them. They had seven children and life had to go on so they would move around each other without words. Sometimes the tension and silent resentment would last for weeks. It would bubble under the surface until the next time a verbal exchange was needed, with the process repeating itself over and over again.

As a child, I watched this verbal sparring and the silent treatment that always followed. Having learned an abundance of wonderful life-enhancing tools from my parents, unfortunately healthy conflict resolution was not one of them. As an adult, I went out in the world equipped with the only tools that I had – verbal explosion or detachment. That explains why, when I had my first adult confrontation with my two college roommates, my default setting was set to go straight to verbal assault. It was what I knew. As roommates, we had already given each other weeks of the silent treatment, which was in me too.

I'm sure that both my parents inherited that from their parents. I was able to confirm that from my Mother as she would share snippets of her childhood and the volatile relationship between her parents. I made a vow to myself that before I got married, I would make every effort to heal that part of my story. I didn't want to bring that part of my history into my marriage and then pass it on to my child. As a continual work in progress, that conscious decision has led me on a 40-year personal development quest. Just when I think that I have completely healed that aspect of my personality, my teenaged son uncovers yet another layer for me to work on. He will mirror aspects of myself that I can't see

- especially when we figuratively bump heads. I can easily recognize the vines that are still on our family tree as they continually manifest in the adult interactions between my siblings. I look at the patterns and how the only path (other than Divine intervention) is conscious awareness and healing to root it out.

I'm grateful that I can literally see shifts in my son as I demonstrate a different behavior, as well as share with him tools that I have learned. I hope that when he leaves our home, he will have new cellular memories as well as a lifetime of positive experiences that he can draw on in his adult relationships; conflict resolution tools that my husband and I have grafted into our family tree through our interactions that will benefit all generations to come. Each time I get it right, my heart smiles and I can feel a lightness of spirit that I know is coming from my father, grandmother, and other relatives who are in the spirit realm. I know beyond a shadow of a doubt that they surround me and my healing is their healing, just as my healing is my son's healing. I stand in the current of continuous spiritual connection that flows both backward and forwards.

When I used to work with teen girls, I would share with them the following analogy: I would have them imagine that I was holding an apple in front of them. I would then cut the pretend apple in half. I would ask them if they would be able to count the number of seeds in the apple if it were real. The resounding response was always *"Yes."* I would then ask them if they could count the number of apples in each seed? Of course, they couldn't, but it always led us into a vibrant discussion about our connection to future generations and our individual and collective responsibilities and legacies. Every living thing creates/produces seeds to ensure its immortality. We come with a desire to activate the seeds within us – through our purpose and our personal mission. We can either choose to activate them or not.

Many First Nation cultures believe in a Seven Generations Principle. Simply stated, it's that every decision we make, whether personal or societal, affects seven generations. And it makes sense if we put it into today's context. For example, many of us know of, or at least have knowledge of, our grandparents and their parents, our parents and our children's children (our grandchildren), and potentially our great-grandchildren. If we don't know our great-grandparents, we can connect to them through family stories, photos, and even mementos or family heirlooms. Those are seven generations (including our own) that connect us within our family line. Just as we can affect future generations, I believe that we can heal the energetic signatures left by preceding generations. We can shift our beliefs to correct wrongs done by previous generations.

> *"We have inherited the color of our hair, eyes, skin and body type, then we must also have inherited the beliefs, thoughts, and memories of our ancestors."*
> – Raymon Grace, healer & teacher

The ties that bind us all are invisible but strong. We all have a genetic susceptibility, having inherited some measure of faulty genes/beliefs.

How do we help heal the souls of generations past and in the future? We have to see where the pain points are and then consciously address them. Often, it can be overwhelming because there is so much pain. We carry all the stories in our collective database. The stories are our shared roots which shape our experiences. What makes 'race' relations particularly tricky, is that the wrongs done in the past have never really been acknowledged as a whole and there is a racist system that is still in place.

The past isn't the past until we get past it.

As a nation, we haven't addressed what we have inherited from our ancestors: inherited fear, anger, mistrust, and trauma. We haven't transformed that energy in mass consciousness, so it remains a barrier to our cross-cultural connections. The trauma that is encoded in our DNA leeches onto our personalities. It is those invisible generational wounds that fuel our inability to trust one another. Thus, most of the information we are responding to is grounded in old data. It is the accumulated memories of the past that haunt us, keeping us perpetually in debt.

The crimes done in the past continue to accrue interest and the payments will never end until the debt is paid or released. Until we feel resolution on both sides of the pain, we will not be at peace because the inherited debt lingers. We have inherited pain, shame, fear, disconnection, denial, sadness, anger, and rage. When we can recognize that much of what we feel is connected to the debts of those gone before us, we can then be of greater service and assistance in our societal healing by consciously resolving them.

We all know the truth of this country's past. If we really want to assist in our collective healing, we need to be ambassadors to stand in for our ancestors. Their souls need healing. Our souls need healing. There are cellular memories that are etched into the fibers of our souls. When we don't heal from the inside, we attack those we perceive are outside of us or 'other.' When we don't heal, we stay in a state of grief and shame that paralyzes us from being active in the solution. However, we can only treat the past wounds that we have access to.

Each individual has access to their family histories as well as their collective consciousness networks. It is a spiritual work that we all can do. We all have mixed heritages with the DNA of many different cultures running through our veins. Due to our sordid past, we have ancestors of various cultures and are more mixed than our outer coverings reveal – sometimes distant and sometimes not so distant.

Their DNA is part of our Earth suits. We are not as pure blood as many would like to think and believe. Our skinsuit may look a specific color, automatically ascribing us to a particular cultural group, but on the inside, the culture that is more aligned with how we feel may be different. It is possible because there has been so much mixing of our genetics. There is cross-cultural ancestral information and pain that lies within each of us. We just have to have the self-awareness and desire to heal it.

All my relations. Even the white heritage that
is also in me whether by choice or by force.

Everyone wants to honor his ancestors. The challenge is that our history is so fractured. Countless black people have shared white ancestors with the cellular makeup activating different memories of the same ancestors. For example, having Alabama and Mississippi family roots, many of my white ancestors who are a part of my family tree are there through force and some in more recent generations, by choice.

My father's mother was multi-cultural. She had a black mother and a white father, which resulted in my paternal grandmother being a very fair-skinned woman with robust Caucasian features. In some settings, she could have definitely been mistaken for white. I don't know the circumstances surrounding her parents (my paternal great-grandparents), but what I do know is that it is not a unique story. Those white seeds that were planted into my family tree created vines that are now intertwined and in need of healing as well.

A few years back, I had the honor of being adopted by an Oglala Lakota family during a sacred, traditional Lakota ceremony. I was in South Dakota co-facilitating a healing retreat that included Red, Black and White women. There was a lot of unspoken trauma in the room. It was difficult for some of the First Nation women as well as the black women, to sit in a sacred circle with white women whose mere presence represented unacknowledged high crimes against them and their families without being triggered.

My spirit pressed me to share a particular healing process with the women. A portion of the process would allow the white women to directly support healing the generational wounds carried by the Lakota women who were in attendance. Some Lakota elders had experienced kidnapping, torture, and forced boarding school when they were little girls, as well as others whose relatives were taken.

The healing process was crafted by Spirit as I followed the gentle whispers in my soul's ears. Without revealing the details of this powerful experience and the identities of the women present, I will say that it required the white women to stand as representatives for their people and with anonymity (it was done in pitch darkness) ask for forgiveness for their dominant cultural ancestors. Many of them were able to do it. It was a compelling and emotional process. There were many tears shed on all sides as huge rips in our cross-cultural fabric were being knit together.

I wish I could say that the process was seamless, but it wasn't. Unfortunately, there was a small band of white women who refused to open their hearts. When I explained to them ahead of time what was going to happen, they all agreed to participate. Once the process began, they went through the motions and pretended that they were 'in' but afterward and when they returned home, they whispered among themselves and to others, hurtful comments like, "*Who does this n*gger think she is?!*" "*I hadn't done ANYTHING, so I didn't apologize!*" "*I did NOTHING to those people to apologize for!*" It was definitely hurtful to hear their response particularly since I had considered many of them friends. If I hadn't been anchored and confident that the process I shared was indeed guided by Spirit, I could have easily matched their anger with my version of defensiveness. Instead, it had no negative effect because I was following the promptings from Spirit that were whispered in my ears – and that was most important to me.

Unfortunately, those few women missed an opportunity to support the Lakota women in their healing specifically and through the very act of witnessing, the healing of all of the women who were present. They forgot that we were all connected. Instead, they focused on our perceived differences and their racialized prejudice against me. They also missed an opportunity to heal themselves and a piece of their cultural and ancestral disconnection. Not wanting to be associated with the adverse actions and behaviors of their dominant cultural group members is why many spiritual beings disguised as white people stay in denial, guilt, and shame.

As a spiritual being, cleverly disguised as a black woman, if I am to be completely transparent, within the black Cultural Network, there are cross-cultural wounds that are specific to white men and injuries that are specific to white women. That distinction is important because there are undercurrents and invisible barriers that prevent trust and authentic cross-cultural relations. One of the most significant ancestral wounds that sabotage some First Nation and black women's ability to wholeheartedly accept white women's ally-ship and sisterhood as a whole is our ancestral cellular memories that are specifically tied to the adverse actions of white women in previous generations.

This is the same ancestral, female Storm Trooper energy that turned a blind eye to the brutal torture and rapes of kidnapped young First Nation girls, as well as the abuse and rape of black, enslaved ancestral women by their husbands, fathers, sons, and brothers. The same ancestral energy that lied about abuses committed by black boys and men, and were complicit in their subsequent brutal beatings, assassinations, and lynchings. They didn't hold their men accountable. They were complicit in the abuse. The same white women who have benefited the most from this colorism war, benefited by being protected and uplifted as the ultimate icon of beauty, while white men are held as the ultimate measure of success. That is part of the truth behind the deep chasm that divides us across color lines as women. That is part of the long chain of pain and mistrust that many are unconsciously grappling with and trying to resolve. This pain rises from the Earth and courses through the cellular memories and literal veins of many of the descendants.

It is an unspeakable trauma. This pain has to be reckoned with and resolved to be in the space of complete trust, love, and authenticity.

Unfortunately, we don't have the flip sides of the stories. We don't know what was in the hearts and minds of those white women (and men) of long ago. We don't know their spiritual histories, nor our own. We don't know what was initially planted within them that disconnected them so profoundly from their spiritually connected selves. We can guess, but we don't really know. We are only left with the fruit of their actions and the barriers to trust that it created. It is our responsibility to know and understand all of our inherited and unhealed parts so that we never go through it again.

We have to heal what is unspoken. The eyebrow-raised look with a side-eyed glance shared between women of non-white cultural heritage and the looks of confusion and self-consciousness among white women are all muscle memory responses. This is part of what we have to heal. This is what we as spiritual beings are here to fix and overcome. To change our collective narrative, we have to overcome our genetically inherited histories. It is the last push in denying our oneness.

The past isn't the past until we get past it.

Let us all take a breath.

White women (and white men as well) may feel that this is unfair: to be a representative for the behavior of others – both the living and the dead. All cultural groups have always operated as representatives for their cultures because many cultures are rooted in the belief that we are all connected and responsible to and for one another.

If we can't speak and hear each other's truth without falling into an overwhelming abyss of anger, defensiveness, shame, guilt, and denial, we will continue to be disconnected, frustrated, and emotionally stuck. We will never rise to the infinite power and possibility that also resides within us through our spirits and souls.

I suppose if healing our ancestral lineage were easy, everyone would have already done it. Sometimes it is difficult for white people to come to grips with the fact that they are linked on the causal side in a long chain of pain and their collective (and many times individual) ancestors, that they love and respect, led double lives. Due to our fractured history, we can have two very different cellular memories of the same ancestors and even events. Like it or not, if your dominant ancestry is white, you are a representative for white people as long as you are wearing the white Storm Trooper Earth suit. Right now our cultural links are highlighted. It is our time to heal. But we can't heal what we are unwilling to acknowledge and feel – especially our collective trauma and shame.

The ironic thing is that the more we don't tell each other the truth with an open heart and receive it with an open heart, the very thing we think our actions are preventing brings it on. Sometimes we think by not speaking the truth it will prevent pain when in actuality the truth is liberating. Not speaking the truth keeps us in bondage, fearful, and disconnected from one another because avoidance is never a productive strategy for positive resolution.

Thankfully during that gathering of women on the Reservation in South Dakota, many women whose dominant ancestry is white could and did stand powerfully as representatives for their collective ancestors. They understood the far reaches of this symbolic act. All those who participated with an open heart were bound together afterward soul-to-soul as sisters, relatives, and friends. We left the room feeling deeply connected, lighter in spirit, with hearts opened much bigger and wider. We needed to acknowledge the proverbial elephant in the room, address it, and heal it. It was a beginning to our authentic cross-cultural relations and the rebuilding of acceptance, respect, and trust.

This path isn't for everyone. We have to be willing to humbly accept our place within our ancestry. We must be willing to not personalize others' pain to the point of acting defensively and taking on the shame and guilt of offenses caused by those in our ancestral cultural line. We are all ambassadors for every group we are a part of.

Because of all of the flammable energy that has been poured into our cross-cultural interactions, like lighter fluid, we all have been the givers and receivers of toxic pain. *Hurt people, hurt people* as the saying goes. We have ALL been negatively molded by an unfortunate past.

We have to be willing to hear and tell each other the truth – all sides of the truth. As spiritual beings, we have a fantastic opportunity to act as cultural diplomats and healing ambassadors. If we choose, we can break generational curses and dysfunctional emotional chains. We can hold space to clear our family's name and the spiritual and emotional debts that have accrued in our cultural groups. But without the truth, there can be no healing.

> *If we stay in pain, we inadvertently pave a pain-
> filled road for our children and their children.*

Much of our cultural crossfire is rooted in the past. Soil that we didn't originally dig and plant – at least not in this lifetime. My mother used to tell me all the time that I had an old soul and often I seemed old enough to be her mother. What if these Earth suits are just that – costumes that we get to wear during our Earth experience? What if they are similar to an astronaut's suit for exploration of our vast universe? When we die, we leave the suit behind. If it is our Divine plan, then we come back through a different womb, many times through the same family line and sometimes, different ones. All of it serves the purpose for us to learn and grow.

What if as spiritual beings we get to try on various costumes depending on what we most need to share and learn? There are so many different intersectional ties that make us who we are – a combination of many different cultures.

The fruits we eat today are the ancestors of the fruits that existed in seasons past. We won't eat the fruit of the future, but our children will eat the fruit of whatever we plant today.

On December 4, 2016, we witnessed a beautiful example of ancestral healing in action. More than 4,000 U.S. military veterans from various branches of service came to protect and support the 15,000 plus Lakota, Cheyenne, and global citizens who had gathered to protect the water from corporate fracking and the Dakota Access pipeline. On that cold and blistering day, an army veteran and peace activist Wes Clark Jr., along with dozens of members of the United States military branches, knelt before Lakota and Cheyenne elders, medicine people, leaders, families, and children, to ask forgiveness for the atrocities committed by the armed forces. Auspiciously, December 4 was also the birthday of Thasunke Witko, also known as Chief Crazy Horse (born in 1841), who was one of the greatest Oglala Lakota warriors and protectors to ever live.

On bended knee with humility and tears in his eyes, First Lieutenant Clark said:

"We came here to be the conscience of the Nation. And in that conscience, we must first confess our sins to you. Many of us, me particularly, are from the units that have hurt you over many years. We came. We fought you. We took your land. We signed treaties that we broke. We stole minerals from your sacred hills. We blasted the faces of our presidents onto your sacred mountain. Then we took still more land and then took your children and then we tried to take your language and we tried to eliminate your language that God gave you, and the Creator gave you. We didn't respect you, we polluted your Earth, we've hurt you in so many ways. We've come to say that we are sorry. We are at your service and we beg for your forgiveness."

Even though I was not directly involved, nor physically in the room at Standing Rock when this occurred, it touched my soul deeply. Through my tears, I could feel a little of the pressure lift. It was a start. A brief beginning. In witnessing, my energy was immediately shifted - reset back to love. I believe that because we are all connected, any time we heal cultural wounds, deep cultural wounds, we remove that energy from the planet. Our souls get a little lighter, as do the souls of the generations that are both in front of us as well as those who are behind us.

> *"We cannot live only for ourselves. A thousand*
> *fibers connect us with our fellow men."*
> – Herman Melville, American novelist

The adverse effect of unaddressed trauma is that we continue to see each other only in representational form – relying solely on visual cues based on the color of our Earth suits. When we heal the invisible threads, it gives us an opportunity to knit our fractured human family back together again, piece by piece, healing all our relations.

"Upon suffering beyond suffering: The Red Nation shall rise again and it shall be a blessing for a sick world. A world filled with broken promises, selfishness, and separations. A world longing for light again. I see a time of Seven Generations when all the colors of mankind will gather under the Sacred Tree of Life and the whole Earth will become one circle again. In that day, there will be those among the Lakota who will carry knowledge and understanding of unity among all living things and the young white ones will come to those of my people and ask for this wisdom. I salute the light within your eyes where the whole Universe dwells. For when you are at that center within you and I am at that place within me, we shall be one." – Thasunke Witko, Chief Crazy Horse, Oglala Lakota (born December 4, 1841; transitioning to the spirit realm on September 5, 1877).

> *Our humanity hinges on everyone's humanity;*
> *all of our survival is dependent on the survival of*
> *everyone. You never know who has the medicine.*

CHAPTER NINE

✦ ✦ ✦ ✦ ✦

LEVELING UP:
RAISING OUR VIBRATION

"The secret of change is to focus all of your energy,
not on fighting the old, but on building the new."
– Socrates, philosopher

To be good ambassadors of our cultures, we have to be good representatives, period. How can we tap into that part of us that is our best selves? What trips us up the most is that we forget we are spiritual beings. Many are on a quest that usually starts in their teen or young adult years to uncover, discover, and find their true selves. During that quest we are always trying to make sense of this reality while also living fully in the remembrance of who we indeed are. Until we are solidly grounded on that path, we are many times incongruent with the person we ideally aspire to be, versus who we are in our day-to-day interactions.

There is an old saying, *"When two people meet, there are really six people present; each as they see themselves, as the other person sees them, and as they really are."* Well, I have affectionately renamed these three aspects of ourselves: the Representative, Mirror Me, and our VIP.

The VIP (Vibrationally Intelligent Perspective) is the part of us that is pure love. It is who we really are. The divine center of our being. The aspect of us that we see and remember when we look into the face of an infant – innocent, pure, honest, creative, completely authentic and full of light. It is the truth of who we are – a small piece of Divine Source energy – perfect in every way. The part of us that knows we are connected to all things and is in congruence with who we really are.

Have you ever had a conversation with yourself? Who are you talking to? Better yet, who is talking to who? Who is the 'my' that is speaking in the possessive sense when referencing you? The aspect within us that states, *"This is my body." "These are my eyes." "This is my hair."*

It is the real you. We have come to refer to it as our higher self – the God Consciousness that is within us. It is the part of you/me that is at the heart of our souls plugged directly into the Divine Source. The part of us (like that small container of ocean water) that came to this Earth with a specific plan and purpose. The reason we are here is written in our hearts with the invisible ink of the spirit. As individualized expressions of our Divine Source, our Vibrationally Intelligent Perspective knows at its core our Earth purpose. Our challenge is to remember and then fulfill it.

When you know who you are and why you are here
– you can then exceed your wildest imaginings.

If we were to visit another planet in our solar system, we would need space suits. To survive in this world, the VIP needs a protective covering that will allow it to function and survive in an environment that is different from its home; thus we are given a physical body – an Earth suit. Our Earth suits are equipped with a built-in protective aspect that is designed to help us maneuver and survive here on Earth – it is called our ego. It is what makes us human. Our ego came pre-installed in our Earth suit with its only function being to protect our VIP. It is a false Earthbound self that is separate from our VIP. It has a sub-set of personas that are created through our personal interpretation of our life experiences. It is an identity that we create. A Representative self. A persona that we take on – all designed to protect us while we are here. Everyone's Representative ego is customized to meet their individual needs, with the cellular memories of their ancestors coded seamlessly through their DNA.

For instance, many of us have been raised by adult children in emotionally extreme environments. This leaves us with bouts of some sort of emotional and/or spiritual dehydration. Dehydration to the point of memory loss, which makes us spiritually sleepy. We then forget who we really are.

> *Most of our adult life is spent healing the*
> *wounds that occurred in our childhood.*

These early childhood experiences help to construct our self-image – a Representative self. The different voices of our Representatives are developed through our physical experiences. For instance, in our early years, we often have thoughts about ourselves that are reinforced by others that take root within us, helping to develop our Representative self and its many voices that create our internal dialog. Thoughts like:

> *"I'm not good enough."*
> *"I'm better than you."*
> *"Life isn't fair."*
> *"I never win anything."*
> *"Nobody likes me."*
> *"I'm the best-looking person here."*
> *"My nose makes me ugly."*
> *"I'm glad I'm not them."*
> *"I'm definitely the smartest person in the room."*

It is a never-ending stream of judgments, thoughts, statements, and beliefs that play an immense role in creating our internal dialog, inner turmoil, and emotional drama. Our Representative (ego) hides behind the *"I"* and *"Me"* in those thoughts, judgments, and declarations about our identity. It is all concocted and based on our intellect and the views, experiences, and beliefs of others that we accept as truth. In the center of it all is our Representative, which acts as a protective barrier – filtering, blocking, interpreting, and preventing us from living our lives in truth and with an open heart. And as a result, we cannot claim our God-given powers in their fullness. Our Representative is our internal defense system developed mostly to protect us from real and/or perceived emotional and physical trauma that we experience at the hands of our parent's Representatives, as well as the Representatives of everyone we have encountered along the way.

Our '*inner child*' is not who we really are either, but rather the spiritually and emotionally stuck parts of our '*self-image.*' It is just another aspect of our Representative self. It is a collection of dynamic memories of who we think we are and all that we have experienced that is placed in the time capsule of our minds and shapes our identity. Many of our inner child beliefs are comprised of incomplete information that is often flawed. Our inner child shows up as that part of us that needs healing (i.e., our immaturity and neediness). Our inner child is composed of all of the stories we tell ourselves about our past (particularly our childhoods). Sometimes when we are in a playful, joyously creative frame of mind, we think we are expressing our inner child. In actuality, we are living through our VIP. Our VIP is the divine energy within us that carries the innocence of a child (in its purity) and the creative footprint of our Divine Source.

The voice of our multi-dimensional Representative blares nonstop judgments, beliefs, thoughts, and perceptions about ourselves and everyone else to protect us from any perceived danger —even harm that is self-imposed. The downside is that it prevents us from really living and seeing the truth of who we are. In its feeble attempt to protect the light within us, our Representative covers our light energy instead. And in the dim light of our being, it becomes more and more difficult to remember our divine purpose and see the truth of who we are. We walk around spiritually dehydrated allowing our dark sunglass wearing Representative/Body Guard to act on our behalf.

In this toxic and unsafe world, the VIP in most cases can't just walk around unprotected. We have all developed sub-conscious strategies to empower our Representative and protect our VIP. The Representative is like a built-in security brigade. There is a swat team of Representatives within each of us that provide different levels of protection. Each acts as our front line of defense whenever there is a threat (real or perceived). We develop this aspect of ourselves strictly for protection. Different aspects of our Representative's core create different dialogs within our heads. For example, there is the voice of our Body Guard Representative, Skeptic Representative, Fearful Representative, Confused Representative, Victim Representative, Press Secretary Representative, and our Vulnerable, Innocent Inner Child Representative, just to name a few. Each voice provides a specific layer of protection, as well as steeps us further into the belief that we are separate from our Divine Source as well as everyone and everything.

Usually, around our second birthday, our Representative is developed enough to be recognized and is ready to act and react on our behalf. If you are a parent, you know precisely the moment when your child's Representative self is engaged, because its first word is "*NO!*"

When our son Jelani arrived on the scene, my husband Rod and I were thrilled! While he was our first and turned out to be our only biological child, we've spiritually adopted enough children to have our own gospel choir!

The first couple of years of Jelani's life were truly magical. He was the perfect baby. And then around the close of his first year when he was about to turn two, we noticed a distinct shift in his personality. Our former loving, compliant, agreeable infant, began to change. I remember the exact moment when I met Jelani's activated Representative. He was sitting in his high chair and I was preparing to serve him lunch; food that in prior days he would joyfully eat with no problem. But on this particular day, he decided that everything was unacceptable: the food, the chair, his mother... He began to scowl at me in a manner that I had never witnessed before. If I were to describe it, it looked like a cross between Popeye's facial expression and the incredible Hulk's grimace rolled up in one. This was something new. I called my husband into the room and I presented Jelani a spoonful of his lunch, and again the same facial expression. We knew at that moment – that was his Representative! Since we also knew that Jelani's Representative would be a member of our household for the duration of his Earthly days, we affectionately named him, 'the Face.' Whenever Jelani would give us "the Face," we knew that another level of negotiation had to take place – negotiations that are – with his Representative on behalf of his VIP.

The third aspect is the Mirror Me. When you look in the mirror, what you see is a reflection. It seems real. It is the part of us that reflects others. Just like the moon itself has no light, but is merely a reflection of the sun. I am a reflection of you. The things that I don't like about you are the same things that I don't like about me.

It is in essence "Me, Cleverly Disguised as You." The aspects of me that are a reflection of you. Some have termed it the "you spot it, you got it" part. It's when I see a characteristic in you (usually something that I perceive as a negative quality), and it bugs me because, deep down inside, I have that same unsavory quality. Since a mirror is unable to see its own reflection, it is the part of me that I become aware of and can heal only by being in a relationship with others. It is also the part of us that is rewarded when we seek to do good and support others. When I feel empathy, "your pain in my heart," as I show love, kindness, and support to you, I benefit as well, because "I am you." This is why when you do something nice for someone else, it feels good. The challenging aspect of the Mirror Me part of us is that many times we will seek to help, heal, and support others as a distraction to taking care of ourselves or before first tending to our own needs.

The Representative is our ego-based self and not who we really are. Since our Representative/Secret Service Agent/Body Guard is privileged to intimate, highly classified information about the VIP just by occupying the same physical space, it gets so familiar – to the point that it begins to believe that It knows what is best, real, and true. The Representative communicates through our head and our intellect, wearing the mirrored lenses of the Mirror Me and only sees the world through them. The VIP, however, communicates through our feelings, our hearts, our souls, and in direct connection with our Divine Source.

Our Representative, using its mirrored dark glasses, doesn't realize that when it looks at others, what it sees is itself reflected in others. So it judges that *"It is about them and not me. I don't have a problem, they do. I have to protect myself from them."* Fear. The VIP on the other hand lives and expresses through the heart.

Even though our Representative has access to our heart, it doesn't operate from there. It uses our feelings and emotions to manipulate rather than heal. It is motivated out of fear instead of love. When we are operating through our Representative, our interactions become disingenuous, inauthentic, untrue, fake, and insincere. Our Representative doesn't understand the heart of the matter. It brings confusion, depression, anger, fear, boredom, arrogance, guilt, and shame to situations. The Representative thinks it is way too smart for a spirited, heart-centered approach to any situation. A popular phrase today for many Representatives, when faced with an emotionally uncomfortable situation is to try to shame the other person by saying, *"Get out of your feelings,"* or *"She/He/They are all in their feelings."* As if *'feelings'* themselves were a bad thing.

The good news is that when our VIP (Vibrationally Intelligent Perspective) is empowered and in control, our Representative self has to submit. Our VIP is ultimately in charge and not our Representative. Truth be told, our VIP doesn't really need the Representative for protection at all, because we have within us a built-in guard dog called Intuition.

Our Intuition is the part of our VIP that is our internal spiritual voice. It is an internal compass or GPS system that will always point us in the proper direction; it is our own personalized internal navigation system that leads us back to center – if we heed its prompting. When we live our lives with our VIP in the lead guided by our Intuition, we can never go wrong. It is when our fearful Representative persona is in charge that our lives spin out of control and we feel less and less like our true selves.

Now, this might sound a bit schizophrenic to some, but we actually are designed this way to keep us sane! When a person's Representative has no connection to or is not integrated with their VIP or Mirror Me, they can become narcissistic and/or psychopathic, having no regard for others. At best, we are the most balanced, grounded, and empowered when we have an awareness of the different aspects of our being that can both motivate us to achieve greatness as well as sabotage our every move.

Again, our Representative self is a projection of who we are. I love the movie *The Wiz* as well as the original version, *The Wizard of Oz*. It gives one of the most memorable depictions of the Representative energy that readily comes to mind. The great and powerful Oz was a scary, over-the-top projection (Representative) designed to keep people from knowing the truth of who he was – an utterly non-threatening individual.

Now, what does all of this have to do with healing our cross-cultural divide? If we become aware of these three major aspects of our selves, I believe it could be integral to our growth and evolution. Understanding who we are gives us an opportunity to do the inner work that we each need to do to heal. We can consciously allow our true self (VIP) room to lead us on a path to healing and reconciliation that our Representative self cannot because it does not have the capacity; vulnerability is seen by our Representative as weakness. Vulnerability strips away the illusion of perfection. When we are defensive, we are saying in essence that *"You don't have a right to be angry or displeased with my behavior. I am perfect – just ask my internal attorney."* The goal for any attorney is to win.

Our minds can justify any behavior (cheating, lying, murder, etc.). The Representative goes over the information repeatedly as any good defense attorney would. His/her job is to win the case regardless of fact, guilt or innocence. Even if we are guilty, we still want to win by having a good attorney.

When we look at each other cross-culturally, many times all we see are our Representatives. Our sordid past keeps our Representative selves front and center. It is our protective layer. I judge that the women who refused to be vulnerable during the healing process in South Dakota were led by their Representatives. Their actions were a form of self-protection. A hypervigilant Representative is usually a telltale indicator of someone who has been wounded or hurt in the past. Remember, we come here as babies – vulnerable with open hearts. It is only through our human experiences that we learn to shut down aspects of ourselves to "*protect*" ourselves.

Insults only hurt if it confirms something that
we have said or are saying to ourselves.

That vulnerability is only possible when we allow our VIP to lead us and not our Representative self. Our VIP, because it is, in essence, a small container of Divine Source, can tap into a larger pool of higher frequency energy because that is what it is. When you raise your vibration to the level of Divine Source, you can then see the connections to all things. You may not understand all of the intricacies, but your awareness shifts. You see the Divine Will in all things. You begin to see, and hopefully realize, that there are no tragedies because even death itself is not real. We are eternal beings having a human experience. We are here to heal the aspects of us that are not in vibrational harmony with our Creator, learning all kinds of individual and collective lessons along the way.

Every situation gives us an opportunity to either see and experience it through the protective lenses of our human Representative self, or our divinely centered VIP. When I look at you as an extension of me, then I am more apt to expend the energy to understand rather than condemn. It goes beyond the fake self-love generated by our Representative self. I call it phony love because many of us have an extremely abusive relationship with ourselves. Our internal dialogues can be brutal. Some people are in a painful and abusive relationship with themselves. They beat themselves up, saying all kinds of mean and degrading things, participating in a toxic inner dialogue:

Man, I am so stupid. I can't believe I just said that! I'm such a mess! I can't do it. People won't like me. I never follow through. I'll never be any different. It won't work. I'm not good enough. I should____, I'll never be____, I'm such an idiot! I'm nothing compared to those people. I look a mess. I can't believe I just said/did that! There's no point. I have to be perfect. Why does this always happen to me?

A constant barrage of negative self-judgments that are effortlessly generated by our Representative self. It is conditional love and this is precisely why many times we can't give or receive unconditional love; we don't show that kind of love even to ourselves.

Out of the abundance of the heart, our mouths speak. You can't give what you don't have. You are what you eat. All of these sayings we use as clichés, but they are correct. Our VIP is always in direct conflict with our Representative self that continually focuses on our human shortcomings. Our VIP is continuously reminding us that we are worthy.

I am reminded of a short parable that has been attributed as a Native American story. A wise elder is teaching his grandson about life:

"A fight is going on inside me," he said to the boy. "It is a terrible fight and it is between two wolves. One is evil. He is anger, envy, sorrow, regret, greed, arrogance, self-pity, guilt, resentment, inferiority, lies, false pride, superiority, self-doubt, and ego. The other is good. He is joy, peace, love, hope, serenity, humility, kindness, benevolence, empathy, generosity, truth, compassion, and faith. The same fight is going on inside you and inside every other person too." The grandson then asked his grandfather, "Which wolf will win?" The elder simply replied, "The one you feed."

The antidote is in all of us; we just have to activate it. We have to put our VIP front and center in our personalities. It is the only part of us that is not vested in this conditional, performance and color-based value system and its byproduct of division and pain.

Our Representative Mind is an unforgiving mind. Forgiveness cannot come through the Representative. The Representative says, *"I forgive,"* then lists the grievances and becomes angrier than ever. Forgiveness is releasing the demand that something (ourselves, others, a situation) is or should have been different than it is or was. It is a release - a letting go. It is the ultimate trust fall. It requires us to 'Level Up' then let go. Allowing our VIP to help us to evolve is a beautiful vision, but how do we make it a reality? It requires self-healing work.

This is where the Mirror Me aspect can be the most beneficial to our growth and self-healing. My Mirror Me, when I engage with you, is an opportunity for me not to get to know you but for me to get to know who I am. For example, my Representative self can make me believe that I am tolerant, loving, inclusive and kind, especially when I am not challenged. I can say all day that I have superpowers – but until I actually use them, what good are they? How can you know who you are if you never have opportunities to exercise and demonstrate your beliefs? Love is active.

The VIP aspects of ourselves are always looking for ways to demonstrate love – both to ourselves and others. It is very present-focused. It doesn't stay tuned in to the Cultural Consciousness network stations mindlessly, it tunes in to higher frequencies and stations that reinforce our invisible connections.

> *"Your perception of me is a reflection of you;*
> *my reaction to you is an awareness of me."*
> – Author Unknown

Our VIP uses the reflective aspects of our Mirror Me to challenge us to truly understand who we are. Let me give you a contrast. Our Mirror Me, under the influence of our Representative, would say, *"What is wrong with him/her/them? They are _____"* (fill in the blank with some negative judgment). Whereas our Mirror Me under the influence of our VIP would say, *"What is it that I am thinking about you that is keeping me from alignment with you? What am I choosing to focus on? And why? Who do you remind me of? What situation is this triggering for me? Am I tapping into someone else's chain of pain?"*

We all have our own personalized curriculums that were pre-selected before we arrived here on the planet. We came here with a purpose and all of our courses of study are designed for our growth and expansion as spiritual beings. The spiritual agenda of our Vibrationally Intelligent Perspective (VIP) is many times very different than our human agenda. Humanly speaking, there is no value in pain, injustice or death, whereas spiritually speaking, suffering, injustice and also perceived death can offer us tremendous opportunities for spiritual growth – a master's level spiritual development course for all who participate, witness, and remember it.

Let me offer an example. Suppose as spiritual beings, in preparation for our time here at the Earth School University, we met with our spiritual advisors. With their help, we decided that what we as spiritual beings needed most in our individual and collective spiritual evolution, was to spend a lifetime learning about 'compassion.' What if the lesson of compassion was a required pre-requisite course for every spiritual being who decided to come to the spiritual college of Earth? What if all of the spiritual classes that we take in our lifetime are lovingly and skillfully designed to teach us various aspects of compassion? Courses that give us opportunities to exhibit, demonstrate, model, contemplate, and dissect all of the many facets and angles of compassion until we not only know it, but we ultimately become it.

"Nothing ever goes away until it
teaches us what we need to learn."
– Author Unknown

Change never happens in the middle. You have to move beyond complacency and nonchalance. Sadness, anger, love, and fear are powerful emotions that evoke transformation. By consciously giving our VIP the space to transcend our perceived Earth suits, we shift not only our vibration, but the vibration of the world. As we raise the world's vibration, we experience and witness a revolution of thought, mind, and spirit - a revolution of the soul.

We have to look into the spiritual eyes of every being (that is cleverly disguised in their colorful Earth suits), until we see the face of our Divine Source. As we look, we will either see our greatest fears or our highest potential. It will disgust or inspire us. No matter what we see, it is all designed to evoke change within us.

Level Up to your true VIP status.

CHAPTER TEN

GETTING RID OF THE MALWARE

*We have forgotten our original instructions. The rest
of the planet – nature and animals - have never
forgotten their original instructions and purpose.
Humankind is the only one who needs to be rebooted.*

When we arrive here on the planet as babies, for the most part we are divine perfection, happy, and loving. Babies smile and respond positively to love (unless there is some physical or mental challenge or disease). All they want is to be loved, fed, protected, and of course, kept dry. They come here with a tremendous capacity for love, and we love being around them. So, how can we like babies and hate people? Well, for one, babies offer no resistance. They don't carry painful backstories that cloud everything they say, see, do, and feel. Babies live in the moment; they cry because of pain at the moment and not over past hurts. They are easily distracted because they are present focused. It's all about the *'now.'*

So, what happens to us as we age that makes us not so loveable? Well, we certainly pick up tons of mental and emotional debris along the way such as thoughts, behaviors, and beliefs that we collect through our environment, families, cultural groups, and the world. We receive it then it resonates throughout our entire being - almost like a virus in a computer program. Just like a computer, you have to update the software and then reboot. Reset the suit.

We love babies because there is no history in their browsers; no malware or corruption in their Source Code. They are unaware of cultural difference and attach no intrinsic value to skin color; they only begin to notice cultural differences and their effects between the ages of 2- 4 years. Throughout their childhood, they are bombarded with stereotypes, misinformation, and lies about 'race' and other cultural aspects.

Like a computer, each of us has to look within and see where our internal systems have been corrupted and compromised. We have to locate the places within ourselves where malware is running or where our wires have become so frayed that they are short-circuiting our system. In service to humanity it is our individual responsibility to rewire our suits. We have to reset our own Earth suits back to their original Divine Source Code setting.

How do we recalibrate the world, optimizing our individual operating systems? Over the years, I have certainly had my fair share of computer challenges. My husband is a computer software engineer and has shown me things that I can to do to help restore my personal computer to its optimal performance when it is on the brink. These same principles can also support us in ridding ourselves of the malicious coding of racism that runs through our own Earth suit computers like a virus.

Reboot. Many of us get frustrated because here we are back in the same energy of the 1950s and 1960s. It feels like Deja vu – because it is. We have been here before both collectively and individually. It's not exactly the same because we are not exactly the same. We keep recreating the program that we are stuck on. Like a video game, you get an infinite amount of opportunities to complete a level. Each day, you can go back to that level and the program will restart it or put you back to where you last left it. How do you level up? The longer you play, the better you get, and the further you can go. You level up.

I used to like playing strategy games on my phone. Sometimes I would install them on my phone and mindlessly play whenever I wanted to relax. As I moved up to higher levels, I would inevitably get stuck on a more difficult one. Sometimes, after several attempts to complete the challenge, I would delete the game from my phone then reinstall it. Why? Because when I did, something about being able to restart energized me and I would get better at it and move through the levels quicker and with higher and higher scores. Each time I restarted, I gained wisdom and experience and got better.

Cultural healing comes from us rebooting our internal genetic hardware and software. All modern day cultures that have been infected and affected by racism have things to heal. We have to repair the wounds, scars, and all the other physical manifestations of history. The old programming and outdated software, if it continues to go unchecked, becomes the malicious codes in our systems. The most significant resistance we can offer to racism and prejudice is self-knowledge and self-healing. Recognizing that our systems desperately need to be rebooted is the first step because you can't heal what you are unwilling to feel and you can't fix what you don't see as broken.

*Let's step out of the story. Reset the
game so we can Level Up.*

Clear your cache. Just like with a computer, our internal cache stores data. When we meet someone of a different ethnic or cultural background, often we will use the information that we already have cached about her cultural group. Caching makes it easier to access information that is stored in our Collective Consciousness network and in our subconscious, making our ability to stereotype, discriminate, and generalize others effortless. Caching makes our snap judgments and unconscious biases faster to internally process. It makes it easier to reload previously generalized information, again and again, keeping the past ever present. Every cross-cultural injustice is cached. It is a natural retrieval mechanism that when left unchecked, will eat up all of your RAM (Readily Available Moments). It leaves no room for new experiences, keeping the same narratives and storylines running. Like a default setting, it requires no effort to maintain.

If we want to have different experiences, we have to clear out our cache from time to time so that we can take advantage of the Readily Available Moments. We have to get rid of unwanted information that is slowing down our operating systems and expand our circle to include people who are of different cultures and backgrounds from us. We can easily miss those moments of authenticity cross-culturally when we prejudge and stereotype.

One way to effectively clear out our cache is mindfulness – being present, focused, and aware of the many filters and snap judgments that we make each time we encounter a new person or experience. We have many painful memories stored and it is effortless to place others in storylines that we have had in the past. Asking simple questions like, *"What is unique about this person or situation that I am potentially missing or overlooking?" "I initially don't like this person. What person or incident am I subconsciously linking them too?" "Have I pre-judged them or treated them in an unconsciously biased way?"* Through whose eyes do you see the world? Your parents? Your grandparents? Your third-grade teacher? Clear out your cache.

Delete programs that are obsolete. Typically, there is a bevy of outdated and obsolete programs that eat up our memory. Often, we talk of the past as if it were the present and treat every situation the same. When we run outdated programming, we tend to make inaccurate assumptions and stereotypical judgments. For instance, as I mentioned in a previous chapter, many of us were taught that we were different races. When we continue to refer to each other as such, it is like running obsolete programming. That false teaching was ingrained in us in school with a passing grade hinging on our ability to regurgitate it. There is very little that we have been taught in school, particularly when it comes to history and our cross-cultural interactions, that doesn't beg for us to re-examine it. Some things have been falsified, misrepresented, and intentionally omitted that we have learned and internalized. All of the monolithic narratives that have been created as a representation of entire groups of people are obsolete and need to be deleted. It runs the gamut from all sectors and sides: from sexism to classism to ageism to every phobia and prejudgment we entertain and then ingrain to become inflexible facts. They become virtually impossible to delete if you aren't even aware that the program is running in the background.

> *"In all affairs, it's a healthy thing now and*
> *then to hang a question mark on the things*
> *you have long taken for granted."*
> - Bertrand Russell, philosopher

Limit how many programs run upon startup. When you wake up in the morning, do you take time to ground yourself, or do you pick up your phone and immediately plug into social media and/or the news feeds? Allowing yourself to become centered and grounded before plugging in can do wonders.

I had allowed myself to get into the habit of checking my phone when I first woke up in the morning. Having it right next to me on my nightstand made it very convenient to check emails, social media feeds, and the news in general as soon as I opened my eyes. Over time I realized that a considerable amount of time had passed and I was still scrolling while in the bed, getting sucked into the endless feed of information. One social media post or video would seamlessly roll into another, eating up my precious time first thing in the morning. What I also noticed was that it would shape my mood. I would start the day with yesterday's news repositioned in the front of my mind, cheating me out of the fresh start that each new morning generously gives. It tricked me out of remembering and processing my dreams and the whispers from spirit that come in the wee hours of the morning.

When I became aware, I started plugging my phone in an outlet on the other side of the room, forcing me to get out of the bed to access it. It gives me the opportunity to make a conscious decision as to how I will start my day rather than to just mindlessly plug in. Moving my phone those few extra feet affords me the opportunity to plug into Divine Source first thing in the morning to listen, download new information, journal my thoughts, and reflect on all the things that I am grateful for. I get grounded. I remember. Sometimes I fall back into my old habit, but when I make that tiny shift in the morning, it makes a significant change in my day. The more I do it, the more I want to do it. It is one way that I have found to stop programs from automatically launching as soon as my conscious computer-like brain gets turned on.

Update software and operating system. There are some programs and functionalities on my computer that are not even accessible to me unless I upgrade my operating system to the latest version. Not doing so limits my capability and creates a path for hackers and viruses. Are you running an old version of history? Toxic and divisive narratives repeat themselves because we don't take into consideration that things are changing. Even though some of the divisive rhetoric that is prevalent in our culture sounds familiar, it isn't exactly the same. Fears that everything will remain the same are not realistic because the world is changing. We can't even access the new and improved version if we are stuck viewing the world through old and outdated lenses.

I remember back in the 1970s when Motorola released what was the latest technology at the time - the first mobile phone for vehicles. They were these big bulky CB radio like gadgets that were status symbols because everyone couldn't afford them. At the time, they were so popular that some people had them installed in their cars and would pretend to be on the phone while driving just to show them off. Once, I was riding in a car with a friend who had just installed one. He was so proud to show it off but couldn't afford the cost of maintaining the phone service, so he would just pretend to talk on it. It was hilarious. Today, if that technology were installed in our modern vehicles, it would be laughable and utterly useless.

Technology is advancing at a speed that is difficult to keep up with and just when you think you have the latest version of something, sometimes before you can even get it out of the box, an updated version is released. Technology is continuously evolving; and like technology, so are we.

We are advancing in all areas of learning. The information in school textbooks that were written back in the 1970s, '80s, and '90s is for the most part obsolete. Much of the data is no longer valid and grossly outdated. Like technology, our children are arriving on the planet much more advanced as well; spiritual beings are coming here with upgraded operating system Earth suits.

It is no doubt that each generation is getting smarter and smarter. Younger generations see and move in the world differently. Their advanced capabilities many times mimic the speed of advanced computer processors not only in their ability to master technology but also in how they see and maneuver themselves in the world. One of the things I admire about youth is their ability to challenge long-standing beliefs and constructs more readily than many in older generations. They have energy, fluidity, and drive.

The flip side of it is that the older we become, the more wisdom is available; understanding that only comes with the experience of enduring a painful historical past. Sometimes, it is easier to just struggle through old beliefs and patterns because learning something new has such a big learning curve. It becomes overwhelming, leading to pessimism, depression, and negativity.

Because prejudice, unconscious bias, and privilege are difficult to see, they also are difficult to correct. The only auto-correct mechanism we have can only be accessed through an upgrade in consciousness.

> *"Every man takes the limits of his own field*
> *of vision for the limits of the world."*
> – Arthur Schopenhaur, philosopher

Our Nation is searching for a new story. We desperately want a new story but are stuck in the old, contemplating: *How do we honor our ancestors yet create a different narrative?* Our belief systems have to evolve, then our behavior has no choice but to follow. Unfortunately, there is no magic wand to wave, nor special pills that we can take that will shift us.

The one thing that we can do is realize that our thinking is outdated and admit that there is a ton of stuff that we don't know, nor have access to, because of our antiquated operating system and concretely embedded beliefs.

All areas need to be upgraded: Our educational, religious, health, governmental systems all need an overhaul. These systems are all powered by human energy. If we individually update our thinking it will fire through our Collective Consciousness networks and old outdated information and beliefs would eventually be rendered inoperable. Many of them already are, but the past energy that was previously deposited in them has not run out or rather run its course. We just have to stop adding fuel to the old and turn our attention to the upgraded thinking that runs through our society that is working. We either have to upgrade or get left behind in a monochromatic, divisive, analog mindset, missing out on a more multicultural, unified world experience.

Increase your memory. The way to expand anything is to increase its allotted space. As spiritual beings in these colorful Earth suits, we have limited capacity. For instance, my physical body can only contain a finite amount of food. If I try to eat more than I am able to digest, my body will get sick and it could eventually kill me by overtaxing my internal systems.

We all have limited capacity in our humanness, but unlimited ability when we tap into our spiritual selves. As a spiritual being, I have access to information that far exceeds my comprehension and understanding. There is a wealth of spiritual knowledge; information that I don't know and don't even know that I don't know. With a computer, all you have to do is type in a question or better yet, ask all-knowing Siri or Cortana, and voila! – the answer magically appears. In our humanness, we have to make room within our beings to receive new spiritually sourced information.

There is an abundance of good that is available in our society. There has been much progress made across cultures, but if we can't receive it individually, it is useless to us. If for instance, you want to be in a position to see and demonstrate more love cross-culturally, you must first create the space by eliminating some internal fear. We all have the same capacity.

If feelings of anger and fear are taking up vital space within you, you have to increase your memory. Creating positive cross-cultural experiences expands us. During challenging times, when we have more positive than negative memories to draw on, we are less likely to generalize people. We are less likely to make them a representative for the entire group when we expand ourselves by adding more positive personal experiences to our memories.

My experience with my second college roommate increased my internal memory. Together, we created positive memories that counterbalanced the negative experience I had with my two previous roommates. I had to increase my internal memory to accept her as a unique individual and not a representative of all white people. That shift in consciousness expanded us both. The payoff to adding more memory is that each time we open our hearts and minds to others who don't mimic our perspective – our hearts expand.

> *"The more my heart expands, the less offended*
> *I feel by other people working out their*
> *particular stage of being a human."*
> - Author Unknown

Shut down and restart (at least) once a week. When you continually leave your computer on, background programs and applications hog its memory. The same thing happens with our internal computers. Shutting down, or restarting, refreshes your memory. Unplugging and reconnecting with nature helps us to remember our connection and the beautiful co-dependent relationship we have with nature and Mother

Earth. Powering down through prayer, mindfulness, meditation, and reflection, are some of the fastest ways to power up. We can then move through this world with more clarity and ease when we are refreshed in our hearts and minds.

Check for frayed wires. Locate the disconnection then rewire back to The Source Code, which ultimately connects us all together as one. Whenever we think of someone as the '*other*,' we have cut wires of continuity, yielding actual tangible effects. When we don't see our connection to everything, it is easy to walk in a way that cuts others off. When we do, it is like cutting off an appendage. It is a self-inflicted wound, and your entire body would suffer.

We are all part of the same body. It becomes challenging to actualize when we become inflexible to change and intolerant of difference.

Language is a vibration we speak and then act out of. Anytime you say, "*That's just the way I am*," you are fighting for your limitations and matching that vibration.

If your beliefs have calcified, there is no room for evolution. Evolution requires flow, a steady stream of new energy, which is difficult to achieve when we are not fully connected. Check for blockages and places where your energy is stuck or disconnected.

Get rid of the malware and empty the trash. There are so many things that we need to release that are hard to let go of. I wish that our cultural differences could be eliminated as quickly as dragging them to the trash like on a computer. As I stated earlier, racism is like a virus that has infected and affected all of our internal systems. Many times we have thought patterns that are full of malware with malicious codes. Most of us don't take the time to examine and reevaluate all of the preconceived notions and beliefs that we have running in our minds. There are a lot of Junk files to wade through. All spiritual beings, when you come here, inherit an Earth suit with a Junk file folder. Through normal living, you can easily become mentally, emotionally and spiritually cluttered with thousands of Junk files; some you inherited and some you collect along the way. SPAM: **S**uperficial **P**rejudgments **A**gainst **M**ankind. Colorism is SPAM. What could be more superficial than prejudging a person based on the color of their Earth suit?

There is no way to eliminate these prejudgments unless we are intentional. We have to do our healing work. Like corrupt files on a computer, implicit bias, prejudice and discrimination are often hidden in plain sight and they don't just magically disappear. You have to intentionally remove them.

Computer hackers know how to mask files and even websites to make you think that they are legitimate when they are not. You have to understand what you are looking for to detect and remove malware. We have all been infected by our shared dysfunctional history. Our human-computer systems are not all the same, so how we treat corruption is different as well. We can support our collective emotional health and well-being by just knowing that we all have corrupt files that need to be discarded. The contents of our SPAM folders are different; our prescriptions for healing are different. Each piece of malware has to be examined and eliminated. It is a tedious process, but once you know the characteristics of corrupt files, it becomes easier to see them and get rid of them. That is the work. Everyone has to make the choice of what to keep and what needs to be thrown away. We have lots of SPAM to go through, both individually and collectively.

Just like with my computer, I can put a file in the trash, but it doesn't leave my computer. I have to take the extra step of emptying the trash to send it back out into cyberspace and permanently off my hard drive. A good percentage of our society has made the declaration that the fundamental elements of racism should be thrown in the proverbial trash, wanting structural racism to be eliminated. The challenge is that we haven't emptied our collective trash. When we remove it, we will all know it because our world will feel different and be different. We have over 600 years of Junk files that need to be purged. We are getting there. Just keep dragging files to the trash and pressing for our society as a whole to permanently delete them, creating internal space for external transformation.

CHAPTER ELEVEN

RECLAIMING OUR TIME

*You can't dictate the amount of time it takes
to heal. Healing is quickened sometimes when
a different behavior is demonstrated.*

California State Senator Maxine Waters, (affectionately known as "*Auntie*" Maxine) across the black Cultural Consciousness network, made the statement "*Reclaiming my time*" during a judicial hearing when she was constantly being interrupted by some white male senators. Each time she was interrupted, she would state, "*Reclaiming my time*." I think her words resonated with so many of us because it spoke to what many of us feel. It wasn't just a reclamation of her time at the moment, but a reclamation of time that resounded across the network. Her words hit many black people in a way that we all understood - the deep place from within that her words were expressing. A reclamation of our cultural time.

Right now, many want diversity and inclusion - a way to demonstrate that we as a Nation have moved beyond our tumultuous past. On the other side is a genuine part of us that wants to (before we move on) reclaim the history that was stolen, dismissed, minimized, terrorized, cheated, and scorned. It wants to reclaim the parts of us that we were forced to assimilate to survive. Reclaim our roots. Reclaim the right to choose. Reclaim our bodies – our hair, our skin, our features. Reclaim our time that was spent apologizing and minimizing. Reclaim our languages and ancient rituals. Reclaim our time spent in darkness and fear. Reclaim our time. We just need a minute. In our humanness we are beyond tired, we are exhausted. We are reclaiming our time for self-care. Cultural healing. Regrouping.

"When the roots are deep,
there is no reason to fear the wind."
– African Proverb

Spiritual beings wearing the white skin colored Earth suits have had hundreds of years in this country to really stack up on their collective self-esteem. Our society is designed to be (and is) an affirmation to everything white. Other cultures haven't had that. We all want to be whole. And this part of our healing is very personal and intentional.

For once, collectively, it is not coming from a space of reaction or defense. It is resonating from a much broader and deeper place of love and appreciation. We haven't had time. That is why, for many, the movie *Black Panther* was so phenomenal. It reminded us of the possibility, strength, and creativity that echoes in our being – the sacred secrets our culture, and every culture, hold that unlocks hidden aspects of our Divine Source that we can tap into. We were reminded of our grace and power. We were reminded of our vibrancy, value, and love.

In our secret spaces, we remember all of the wisdom that is stagnated within our DNA. The gifts that we came here culturally to share. We are reclaiming our time to remember, fortify, reconcile, reconnect, and empower. We are reclaiming our roots by planting our spirits back deeply into our cultures.

Only when we are rooted can we share our fruits.

Culture is a shared experience for a group of people and it is a provocative thing. We can't move forward if we pretend that culture hasn't been misappropriated, denied, and stolen. Histories that Indigenous Americans and Africans in America were physically forced to denounce to fit into the white culture. Many are now uncovering their genetic roots, searching to find the specific lineages of their Earth suits, reclaiming all of the information that was lost, and remembering all of the languages that were forbidden to be spoken.

I am reminded of a story that I heard many years ago that is attributed to the Himba people of Namibia in Southern Africa. It was recently brought back to my remembrance by my dear sister friend and storyteller, Nancy Basket. She filled in the blank spaces that I had long forgotten:

"The birthdate of a child is fixed. It is not the time of its arrival in the world, nor in its design, but much earlier: It is the day the child is thought of in his or her mother's mind.

When a woman decides she's going to have a child, she settles down and rests under a tree. She listens until she can hear the song of the child who wants to be born. And after she has heard this child's song, she comes back to the man who will be the father of the child and teaches him that song. And then, when they make love to physically design the child, they sing the song of the child, to invite him or her into this realm.

When the mother is pregnant, she teaches the song of this child to the midwives and older women of the village. So, when the child is born, old women and people around her sing the child's song to welcome the new being.

As the child grows, the other villagers learn the child's song. So if the child falls, or gets hurt, he or she always finds someone to pick them up and sing their song. Similarly, if the child does something wonderful, or successfully passes through the rites of passage, the people of the village sing their song to honor them.

In the tribe, there is another opportunity where villagers sing for the child. If at any time during his or her life, the person commits an aberrant crime or social act, the individual is called in the center of the village and the people of the community form a circle around him or her. Then they sing their song.

The tribe recognizes that the correction of antisocial behavior does not pass through punishment; it is by love and the reminder of one's identity. When you recognize your own song, you don't want or need to do anything that would harm the other.

And the same way through their lives, in marriage, songs are sung together. And when, getting old, this child is lying in her bed ready to die, all the villagers know the person's song, and they sing, for the last time, her song."

We are taking the time to listen to and tell our stories, remember our songs, reclaiming ourselves in the process. Through our songs and stories, we remember who we are. They link us together in a cosmic dance, awakening our souls through each pulsating, rhythmic beat. Rekindling the flame ignited in our spiritual centers.

Right now, we are finding and creating a balance between collaboration, assimilation, and equity while learning that we can do multiple things at once. Yes, we can continue to do cultural sharing, but right now many are trying to remember. We are reconnecting with our original languages, customs, religions, and cultures. It is through those cultural roots that we remember our spiritual connections, our songs, and our connection to the Earth. It is in our connections with the Earth and our origins that we recognize our relationships with all of humanity.

I can love me without hating you. I can
be with you without becoming you.

There are some things that each cultural group has to do for itself. Ethnicity is important because it is your cultural group that defines you. They know what you know. They share your history, your joys, frustrations, and pains in ways that are impossible to explain. Culture is the vehicle that we use as spiritual beings to express ourselves. Cultural expression, in its fullness, is a gift to the entire world; an undeniable demonstration of divine presence. You can feel it when you close your eyes and listen deeply to the rhythmic heartbeat of a drum. Each culture's drum beat is different. Different songs, stories, and dances.

Different expressions but the vibration of the drum is what connects us without words – uniting us beyond our differences. Culture is our very lifeline to our Divine Source. It is how we communicate spiritually. An unspoken language that resonates in our souls.

Right now, many are experiencing spiritual glitches because our wires are fraying and have not had the opportunity to emote and heal without the input and influence of white culture. It is internal healing that is happening within our Cultural Consciousness networks both individually and collectively that is helping us to reclaim ourselves. We are reclaiming the time by putting on our oxygen masks and breathing in our wholeness. This wholeness can only be liberated through the gifts of our cultural expression. Gifts that each group freely shares with all of humanity through our style, food, art, music, creativity, voice, wisdom, intellect, dance, language, laughter, joy, expression, rituals and traditions, light, spirituality, and love. We are reclaiming ourselves and filling up our containers with whispers from our ancestors.

It is only through loving ourselves do we have the capacity to authentically love others. It is through the full acceptance of ourselves that we are then able to accept and embrace others. We are unapologetically owning everything about us. We just need a minute to love who we are in our ethnicity and culture and to reclaim our time. We are taking the time to fortify. Our healing quest is one of the most critical aspects of our survival. We are speaking truth to the power that resides within us and decolonizing our hearts and our minds in the process.

We are healing and mending the fractured and broken places within. Tribal healing. Unfortunately, we can't always heal cross-culturally together, because our wounds are different. It would be like going to the hospital. Everyone is not treated the same. There are different areas or sections of the hospital that specialize in various ailments. Our cross-cultural pain is different and has to be treated differently. People in every culture, need to find acceptable ways to express anger, cope with sadness, manage conflict, show respect, demonstrate love and deal with pain. It is through our stories that we heal.

Once our breathing is steady and sure through our VIP (our Vibrationally Intelligent Perspective), we can and will rejoin the circle. We already come in and out of the bigger circle. Once we remember fully and heal ourselves to the point where we are no longer hyperventilating, then we can help others to improve and remember. If we don't take the time, we will have no choice but to continue to filter our painful backstories through our unforgiving Representative selves - with every cross-cultural interaction kicking up a dust storm of our ancestral trauma.

There are also spiritual costs to Whiteness. Many whites have lost connection to their own ancestral spiritual traditions and consequently have come to romanticize (and appropriate) those of other cultures, such as those of First Nation peoples, Buddhist or Hindu rituals and practices.

So, right now, in the meantime, as the world is changing, and you are waiting, if you are wearing a white earth suit and if other cultures can't talk, don't want to speak, don't have the energy nor the words, talk among yourselves. Read. Support one another. Love one another. Forgive one another. Teach one another. Help one another. Slow down. Reflect. Contemplate. Meditate. Pray. Take your time while many are reclaiming their time.

In the movie *Happy Feet*, there is a particular scene where the young penguins gather with their teacher, Miss Viola, at Penguin Elementary to learn the important lesson of finding their heart songs – all by themselves. The greatest gift that is yielded from remembering our soul's song is the gift of significance, the ability to find meaning in work, faith in ourselves, confidence in the value of our lives, inner strength, love, and hope for the future.

CHAPTER TWELVE

LETTING GO IN THE RAIN

"Sometimes the emotions of yesterday are so present
that we can't imagine the greatness of tomorrow."
— Ronee Martin, musical artist

Rain. In the wee hours of the morning, as I lay in bed, I hear the rain outside. It is a steady rain that goes on for hours and hours. Something is soothing about rain when you are sleeping in a nice comfortable bed, snuggled under a bevy of warm blankets. There's a crispness in the air. As the rain continues to come down, it is easy to fall back into a deep sleep.

I didn't realize before moving to North Carolina that it rained so much here. In fact, it rains a lot in the southeast, period. Lots and lots of rain. Sometimes days and days of nothing but rain. It is overwhelming at times, especially when there is so much water that even the Earth itself can't accommodate it all at once. Trees become uprooted, knocking down power lines. The downed trees and moving debris clog up drainage systems causing many areas to flood. It can be really messy when it gets stuck with no place to go.

There is a solemnness about rain. At times it feels almost as if the Earth herself is grieving. So much pain is stockpiled all over this land and especially here in the South. There are deep footprints of pain that are imprinted here.

The rain feels like Mother Nature is shedding the tears we can't; cleansing and remembering through millions and millions of tiny droplets that have been recycled for thousands and thousands of years. Each one is holding memories that are imprinted within each drop…acting as a conduit for our collective grief. Showing us how to let go. Sometimes it can be overwhelming and quite messy. Sometimes it's not nearly enough. Sometimes, it's just right.

Not being able to grieve our past as a Nation has stifled not only our growth but also our ability to authentically connect with one another across cultures in general. We have thousands upon thousands of pounds of unprocessed grief (especially here in the South) that is piled up so high you can feel it in the air. You can feel the energetic signatures of the sins of the past. There is so much unacknowledged and unresolved pain. A pain that is encoded in each tiny droplet of rain that falls.

Now, more than ever, we want to have cross-cultural dialogue. It seems like just when things settle down, something else happens: a church shooting, police brutality, or some social injustice that further reminds us of our skin-deep divide sending us back into our respective spaces to stuff down more of the unspoken pain. The rain continues to fall, and many are lulled back to sleep.

Much of our ancestral pain is carried
in precious urns in our hearts.

I remember when I first went away to college. There were so many things that I had collected throughout my life up to that point. I wasn't quite ready to let go of most of it. Mementos, favorite clothes, photographs, my doll collection, concert ticket stubs…a little bit of everything. Each item was a touchstone for some precious memory, for someone or someplace I'd been. These were tiny droplets of memories that I boxed up, put my name on in permanent marker, and carried down to the basement of our family home.

Over the years, I forgot the boxes were down there. I went on about my life collecting more mementos and memories. The only time I would remember would be when I would visit my parents. And if I had time, I would rummage through the boxes as I strolled down memory lane.

Our ancestral memories are like that as well. Some memories are stockpiled in the basements of our souls; memories that were collected by our loved ones taking up space within us. Likes and dislikes, prejudices, judgments, etc., are all swirling around deep within us. When we see something on the news, some crime committed, for instance, we unconsciously connect it to a story that is already within us.

The older we get, the more stories and mementos we accumulate and remember; the more cross-cultural strife we experience. If it is unresolved, it can easily and effortlessly get stuffed into the basements of our hearts. We put it in the basement with all of the other collected and unresolved pain. Over time, we have boxes and boxes of stored painful manuscripts that we can't seem to get rid of. Stories of war, injustice, abuse, missed opportunities, no opportunities, privilege, hatred, frustration, terror, defeat, and so much more. Those stories swirl around in the boxes in our inner basements. And just like any standing water, it begins to smell.

As the stench rises, we smell fear, judgment, anger, guilt, and shame. All of the stories didn't originate with us, so we don't even know where to trace the scent and how to discard them. They are the stories of our ancestors and family members. Some we have heard. Some were etched inside of us while we were in our mother's wombs. Everything in our lives acts as a cue to a story. Smells can activate both sweet and bitter memories. Certain sounds can activate a memory from when we were five. People, places, smells, sounds, objects, foods, etc., all act as prompts for tiny droplets of memories: Small story droplets that are continuously dripping within us. All of our painful stories swirl effortlessly in the rising waters in our souls. Like anything, over time, we can hardly smell the rotting stench of it, at all.

How do we get rid of all of the painful stories stockpiled in the basements of our souls? We have to be willing to let go. Letting go can be difficult. It can feel like a betrayal if we let go. Just as we are emptying one box, something happens in the news or over the Internet, at work or at the grocery store, adding more droplets to the box. Every box is filled with of all of the things we should fear, be angry or feel guilt or shame over. All neatly categorized for our attorney-like Representative self to mull through to justify why we just can't get over it and come together.

We have become emotional hoarders
– unable to let go of anything.

Too many boxes… too many things have happened… too much stuff. Overwhelmed, we don't have time to sift through it all. We definitely don't have the time nor the energy to go through each of the boxes, item by item, droplet by droplet. It would take too much time. Most of the stuff isn't ours anyway!

There is a wise African proverb that I love: "*Don't let what someone else eat, make you sick.*" Often we want others to let go of things we aren't willing to let go of ourselves. We are stuck in the past – just stuck. We see the world through the eyes of the past; live in the past; want to go back to the past; and act like we are in the past. And what it does (more than anything) is rob us of our present joy.

"If you are depressed, you are living in the past.
If you are anxious, you are living in the future.
If you are at peace, you are living in the present."
– Lao Tzu, Chinese philosopher

I think we believe that once we allow ourselves to let go, pouring some of the collected pain out to be recycled down the drain, we will drown. All of the boxes will break, our insides will be flooded, and our hearts wouldn't be able to handle it all. In fact, the opposite would happen if we would just allow the water to flow.

When it comes to the stockpile of pain and trauma that has been accrued between the red, black, brown, and white cultural groups, we need to grieve. Grieving allows us to release the pressure when there are no words to express the compressed pain - tears for our ancestors. Tears for all of the pain we have stuffed in the boxes in the basements of our souls. When we grieve, we release the idea that we are *only human* and all of our loved ones are *only human* as well.

> *"We must strive to be moved by a generosity*
> *of spirit that will enable us to outgrow the*
> *hatred and conflicts of the past."*
> – Nelson Mandela, former president of South
> Africa and anti-apartheid revolutionary

I wish we didn't have such a strong value assessment attached to everything – even our tears. Tears have a long history of being associated with weakness. We have been told from childhood to either, *"Don't cry"* or to *"Stop crying."* When we cry, others are quick to hand us a tissue to clean ourselves up and to stop it. So many are on the verge of tears. Tucked away under our tough exteriors, just beneath our Representative personas, are tears. Unshed tears for loved ones that are missed. Tears for bad decisions that were made and all the terrible things that have happened to us. Tears for terrible things we have seen happen to others as well as the things that we wish we could redo. Tears for our bodies and the pain that it has and is enduring. So much to cry for. But we don't. We have to be strong. *"Ain't nobody got time for that."*

> *We are all processing accumulated pain that we*
> *inherit and then don't know how to put down.*

Tears are at the bottom of the emotional food chain. It is sold to us as a weak emotion. Boys shouldn't be caught doing it. Real men, definitely not. Women and girls (especially white women) are told they do it way too much. Tears have been shamed, judged, manipulated, and weaponized for so long that we no longer believe that they are even real. Tears can be okay and acceptable only when they are coupled with joy.

When they team up with anger, sadness, guilt or regret, it is a bit too much to take. I hear people say all the time, *"Don't make me cry."* or *"I told myself that I wasn't going to cry."* We defend our right not to cry as if it were the worst thing that a person could get caught doing.

If we look into the eyes of another soulful being, I mean really look at them, eye to eye and soul to soul, the water can rise. It is as if our souls are asking, *"Where in our bodies are we carrying trauma? Where are we carrying others' trauma?"*

Many of us stand out on the periphery, afraid to make eye contact, and by doing so avoid, deny and stuff our tears down to the basements of our souls. We don't comprehend that our collective emotional basements are already flooding with water rising up to the main floor. We won't be able to hold it back too much longer. The levies are about to break with so many people in pain. We can't even think straight. Don't want to feel. Too much to grasp. So we learn to stuff it down and detach, not realizing that plugging up the holes only keeps the water in. We are being flooded from the inside out.

> *"The organs weep the tears the eyes refuse to shed."*
> – Sir William Osler, Canadian physician

We miss out on all of the benefits of our private rain showers. Tears cleanse all of the emotional toxins and sludge that has piled up within us. It allows the flooded areas a way to move the stagnated energy, the pools of unaddressed grief, unaddressed hurt, unaddressed anger. There is so much to weep for. If we keep stoically holding on, trying not to feel, we will all drown.

A healthy way to process our feelings would be to treat them the same way that we metabolize our food: ingest, digest, process and eliminate. When our bodies are healthy the natural flow of processing food is to ingest or take it in, digest it by breaking it down into usable components, and then process it by distributing it to your cells to be converted to energy. Anything that can't be processed is sent through the colon to be eliminated.

For instance, if someone does something that we choose to be angry about, the first thing that happens is we ingest or take in the emotion of anger. We feel angry and then digest whatever boundary of ours we feel was crossed. We then process what action needs to be taken. Next we eliminate the anger by making a decision to either confront, forgive, ignore, avoid, etc. Once we eliminate the anger we make room for another emotion (of our choosing) to be ingested. Just as we get to choose what foods we eat we also get to choose our emotional state.

The unfortunate part about all of this is that we do want authentic relations. But where do we begin? Sitting at the bottom of the emotional food chain with tears is forgiveness. It is hard to forgive. Somehow we have equated forgiveness with weakness as well; being a pushover, spineless, naïve, and certainly weak.

I have seen and read countless stories of amazing beings who have transformed the energy of unspeakable crimes committed against them or someone they love. For instance, not too long ago, back in 2015, the Charleston, South Carolina, church shooting happened at Emmanuel A.M.E. Church. The shooter declared publicly and unapologetically that he methodically committed the crime that was aimed at the vulnerable parishioners, specifically because of the color of their skin and to "*magnify and incite violence in others.*"

Shortly after, many of the surviving loved ones publicly declared their forgiveness of the shooter. Many people who weren't directly involved nor had any loved ones who were murdered there were highly upset. How could they forgive so quickly? I think those family members knew that holding on to the pain and stuffing it into a box that would eventually find its way down to the basement of their souls, would not be a sufficient declaration of retribution for those whom they loved who were killed. They knew that if they didn't forgive, it would create a constant drip that would inevitably cause them to be flooded from the inside out.

Holding on to the pain would only add to all the other painful boxes already stacked up within them. They did the only brave and compassionate thing they could do. They consciously forgave and let go, not for the shooter, but for themselves. Forgiveness doesn't mean that they condone or overlook what the killer did. They realized that forgiveness didn't diminish the love held deeply in their hearts for their slain loved ones. They chose forgiveness because they couldn't forget. Harboring hatred and resentment would only cause damage to themselves. Forgiveness made room to love their beloved ones even more. We have been taught that if we forgive, the other person wins. We then allow the unforgiving energy to compromise our organs. The other person wins as it kills us (literally).

If you think forgiveness is for the weak, you clearly haven't done it. It is hard work and very difficult because many of us are so shut down, emotionally numbing our pain. It takes a strong spiritual fortitude and rootedness to be able to deeply forgive. And we all have that capacity within us. It works best when we activate our spirits and reconnect our souls to the vast ocean of our Divine Source letting the pain flow back up to the heavens where it will be transformed, re-coded and released as droplets of love, grace, and peace. But it can only happen if we let go.

Clearing out the hurts attached to how we perceive the actions of others is mandatory for healthy reconnection and relationship. Our Hawaiian brothers and sisters offer us a simple, and yet profound way to release all of the murky water that is rising in the basements of our souls.

The Ho'oponopono is an ancient Hawaiian forgiveness process that has been shared globally through the healing work of Dr. Hew Lin. It is an active process that was primarily used (and still is) to heal relationships. The word Ho'oponopono, when broken down, comes from the Hawaiian phrase ho'o which means *"to make"* and the word pono means *"right."* So ho'oponopono means *"to make doubly right."* Being in right relationship with both ourselves as well as others. They understood that all healing happens on an energetic level first starting from within. Others reap the benefits as it flows outwardly and is then extended.

One of the things I love about the Ho'oponopono is that it doesn't require the direct presence or participation of anyone other than one's self. Certainly, it can be used to facilitate healing between two individuals once they have aired their differences. But, it can also be powerfully effective when applied to assist our own internal healing. It is a way to let go and move forward. All that is required is our own authenticity, willingness, and a desire to heal. It is an energy shift that is reserved for those who are not afraid to heal and be led by their Vibrationally Intelligent Perspective.

There are several versions and methodologies associated with the Ho'oponopono. Widely circulated is a four-step process:

Step 1. *"I'm Sorry"*
Step 2. *"Please Forgive Me"*
Step 3. *"Thank You"*
Step 4. *"I Love You"*

On the surface, it can appear to be naively simplistic, especially if our smirking Representative self is reciting it. It can ignite similar feelings to those of the women who were reluctantly participating in the healing process in South Dakota that I spoke of in a previous chapter.

The only way that it can be useful is if it is channeled through our Vibrationally Intelligent Perspective. Our VIP is the part of us that is vested in our spiritual healing and reconciliation. It is the part of us that is not held captive by the bounty of pain that is collected within it. It has the perspective of our Divine Source and knows that the only way that we can be airlifted out of our internal floodwaters is to let go of our sinking floorboards and reach for the lifeline that is lovingly suspended above us.

My husband and I have a dear friend, Vandorn Hinnant. He is a visual artist and sculptor, poet, philosopher, author, and a mystic music-making metaphysician. He is the author of "*Hidden Numbers: The Math Art of Vandorn Hinnant.*"

As I continued to muse over this topic and the sky continued its downpour of rain, I called Vandorn. I will share a portion of the conversation I had with him around the subject of healing with the variation of the Ho'oponopono that he has adapted and uses quite effectively.

Niambi: "*Greetings Vandorn. I wanted to ask you a few questions regarding your use of the Ho'oponopono. Do you have a moment?*"

Vandorn: "*Sure. Let's get right into it.*"

Niambi: "*I'm working on the chapter in my book on forgiveness and I immediately thought of you and The Seven Statements.*"

Vandorn: "*It may be one of the greatest challenges for one's personality/ego self to forgive one's self for one's judgments against experiences (in general). Over a period of many years, I have found great aide in the use of the Seven Statements. They are a synthesis of the statements afforded us by Dr. Masaru Emoto ("Messages in Water"), and Dr. Hew Lin (Ho'Oponopono). I added the seventh statement.*"

Niambi: "*What are they?*"

Vandorn:
"*1. I apologize.*
2. Please forgive me.
3. I love you.
4. I appreciate you.

5. I respect you.
6. I thank you.
7. NOW."

Niambi: "*Was there a reason that you settled on seven?*"

Vandorn: "*Each one of those Seven Statements is actually spoken to one of the major seven chakras* in the human body. So we begin with, 'I apologize' at the Root chakra. Then you go to the second chakra (which is the Sacral chakra), and we say, 'Please forgive me.' To the third chakra, which is the Solar Plexus, we say 'I love you.' At the Heart chakra, we say, 'I appreciate you.' And then at the Throat chakra, 'I respect you.' At the Third Eye chakra, we say, 'I thank you.' And finally, at the Crown chakra, we say, 'NOW.'*"

*Chakras are specific centers in our bodies that energy flows through. The word 'chakra' is a Sanskrit word meaning *'wheel of spinning energy.'* Our chakras are literally whirling, powerhouses of energy.

Niambi: "*Can you expound on the significance? Especially when many people believe that when you forgive you are letting go of someone else's debt.*"

Vandorn: "*First we want to understand that when we say 'I apologize' and 'Please forgive me,' we are not talking to the enemy. We are talking to ourselves. If you heal yourself, then everything outside of you changes. Healing is an inside job. And that is where we have to start. We have to start with this understanding; there is no creative force outside of us. Reality is an inside job. We are the determining factor in the outcome. And honestly, until we get there, we are doomed. That is the first step to waking up. We have too much evidence of this. And yet, we allow ourselves to be distracted by all of the disempowering irrelevant stories. And there are a lot of disempowering irrelevant stories, which is where people tend to place their attention and mismanage their attention.*"

Vandorn: "*The bottom line is that nothing can harm us if we know how to manage our attention.*"

Niambi: "*Ok, so let's talk a little about the statements and why you aligned them with the major energy centers (chakras) in the body.*"

Vandorn: "*Each one of these statements is intimately related to the kind of energies we experience in each one of these energy centers. So, with all of the trauma that has taken place across the timeline, for millennia, that is related to the first and second chakras, all of that trauma is attempting to be addressed in the statements, 'I apologize' and 'Please forgive me'.*"

Vandorn: "*We are doing some powerful healing work. And then 'I love you' to the Solar Plexus. It is important to get that message there because you can't get past the Solar Plexus with any healing unless you talk to the Solar Plexus and affirm 'I love you.'*"

Vandorn: "*We have to address all of this long-standing trauma across millennia by going to where the trauma is stored. That is what we are trying to do; go to where the trauma is stored in the body and then address it to let it go.*"

Niambi: "*That is exactly what I am talking about in the book – all of the stored trauma we carry around in our bodies and how to forgive and let go.*"

Niambi: "*So much negative energy can get stockpiled in the Solar Plexus. Whenever anything happens, we make up a story about it. We digest it and filter it through our personal, emotional, and spiritual digestive systems. What we have just eaten then shapes the experiences we have and we experience the world just as we imagine it. We live in the world our minds create. If our bodies aren't breaking down false narratives and stored up cross-cultural trauma and pain, our bodies (physically, emotionally and spiritually) can't properly eliminate it.*"

Vandorn: "*Yes. The Solar Plexus is where much trauma is still stored. It is where so much trauma is experienced because it is migrating from the Root and the Sacral energy centers into the third chakra, and then the heart gets shut down because of all of this trauma rising.*"

Vandorn: *"We say, 'I appreciate you' at the Heart Chakra. That is important because it addresses the internal question of 'how do you feel about me?' The answer is, 'I appreciate you'."*

Vandorn: *"And then at the Throat Chakra, which is the powerhouse for manifestation and articulation, you say, 'I respect you.' 'I thank you' is spoken to the Third Eye Chakra and 'NOW' is spoken to the Crown Chakra. So, if one can actually be in communion with the Crown Chakra - that would be the portal to what we would call illimitability, which includes space and time. It is like a window to the non-temporal and eternity. The word 'NOW' is a way of connecting one's energy to it immediately."*

Niambi: *"How do you use the Seven Statements?"*

Vandorn: *"I use these seven statements as a round. 'I apologize. Please forgive me. I love you. I appreciate you. I respect you. I thank you. NOW'. Going from the root, through the other chakras to the crown and then back around to the root again. Just like what Qigong Master Mantak Chia teaches with the micro-cosmic and macro-cosmic orbits."*

Niambi: *"How can this work with letting go of ancestral trauma?"*

Vandorn: *"We are all co-creating. We are re-creating the trauma of the past by regurgitating it, reliving it, repeatedly thinking about it, rehashing it, re-hating it; all of that stuff. And so we have to find our way out of that conundrum. It requires a tremendous amount of spiritual fortitude and courage to find one's way out of that conundrum because that is the hamster wheel people are on and they don't know they are on it. So they keep saying, 'I hate this, and I have been abused, and so on.' Every time you think about something, you are giving it power."*

Niambi: *"What about all of the crazy stuff that was done in the past by and to our ancestors? How can we forgive and let go using the Seven Statements?"*

Vandorn: *"Imagine this. Go anywhere on the human timeline... anywhere we (as humans) choose not to trust our gut, we are doomed. If we are* conditioned to have fear as the guiding force in our experience, we are doomed. We have to do some serious emotional cleansing and healing. That is why we have to forgive ourselves. We have to forgive ourselves for running the internal victim conversation. We have to forgive ourselves for allowing ourselves to be duped by what we conveniently call the enemy. I don't care how negative others' (the enemy) behavior may be, they are also pawns on the chessboard of life and they don't even know it. I forgive my ancestors for allowing themselves to be duped by the enemy. We have to start someplace within our human timeline with this thing called culpability."

Niambi: "How do you modify the statements to address the ancestral wounds that we carry in our bodies? How do we rephrase the statements to address their pain that we are carrying?"

Vandorn: "Very simply. When we are doing ancestral healing work, we can use these seven statements:
1. We apologize.
2. Please forgive us.
3. We love you.
4. We appreciate you.
5. We respect you.
6. We thank you.
7. NOW."

Niambi: "Thank you for that Vandorn."

Vandorn: "We cannot afford to continue thinking about what has happened to us in the past. We will never get out of that deep hole until we think about where we really want to be; give all of our energy and attention to this and love it up something fierce. That is the power of manifestation that we are not cognizant of as a collective. By default, unconsciously, we keep recreating the same thing. We haven't chosen to wake up to the fact that we can have a different experience by determining how to and where to place our attention – because that is the determining factor… where we place our attention and that we are the 1st cause."

Niambi: "*There are lots of versions to our story and we get to pick a version and then decide to live it through. You can live through the story of being a human or a spiritual being and thus live out a variation of it.*"

Vandorn: "*We have to decide what is more important to us: the experience of our flesh or the experience of our spirit.*"

Niambi: "*Thank you Vandorn for sharing a powerful tool to support us in our healing evolution.*"

Vandorn: "*Anytime Niambi.*"

"*We live in a time when goodness of the human heart screams for re-cognition in every dimension of our collective condition; our relationships with the Earth, the Air, the Water, and one another. The human heart will suffer but so much oppressive conditioning before it rebels and ascends to a normalcy that it knows to be correct in every way imaginable.*" – Vandorn Hinnant (*www.VandornHinnant.com* and *www.lightweavings.com*)

Remember, rain makes the flowers grow.

CHAPTER THIRTEEN

FINDING YOUR SOUL FAMILY

Just because you are related doesn't
automatically mean you are family.

Do you like jelly beans? I love sour flavored jelly beans. Well, the Jelly Belly Candy Company is one of the premier jelly bean makers in the United States. According to their published information, last year alone, they sold enough jelly beans to circle the earth with jelly beans five times! That's a lot of jelly beans! Can you imagine? Just in one year, you could circle the globe five times, just with jelly beans!

So, I guess just to shake things up a bit, a few years ago, the Jelly Belly Company came up with this really unique idea. They decided to create this game called *Bean Boozled*. Do you know about this game? It is absolutely disgusting! It is disgusting because it is so deceiving. They created these jelly beans that look normal, but when you taste them, they taste like...crazy stuff! For example, you think you are eating what looks like a strawberry jam flavored jelly bean, but it tastes like a centipede. Or you pick one that you think is a juicy pear flavor and it tastes like a booger (now, I know everybody needs to work, but I'm just wondering, whose job it is to figure out the chemical composition of a standard booger and then put it in the form of a jelly bean???). And the crazy thing is – people are buying them (clearly, I bought one)!

You think you're going to get one that tastes like coconut and it tastes like a baby wipe. Or chocolate pudding and it tastes like canned dog food! But you know what I really love about this game is that you don't know what you're going to get just by looking at the jelly beans on the outside. You think you will be tasting one thing and you wind up with something completely different – and that's just like people, right? You can't tell by just looking at the outside of someone what kind of person he is on the inside.

Now, please hear me and understand, I am not advocating that you go around licking people on the forehead to find out what flavor they are. This is not literal. But what it means is that to find out what someone's flavor is, you have to engage. You can't just go by the outer covering. The good news is, there are more good jelly beans in the world than bad jelly beans. Just as there are more good human beings than bad ones. There is more to all of us than meets the eye. Everybody that looks like us aren't for us. And everybody who doesn't look like us isn't against us. The gag is – you can't even tell with your physical eyes. Who we truly are can only be discerned through our spiritual eyes.

Every person represents a multitude of different groups – each with their own culture. It's just like in a body, some cells make up the liver, cells that make up the heart, cells that make up the pancreas and so on. Each group of cells is specialized and unique in their function. A cell by itself can be considered unique, but when you place it in an environment with other cells that are just like it, together they create a culture.

People act similarly. Most people, when they are in a group setting, tend to gravitate toward others who are similar to them – physically or externally. When you have a group of young people for instance, the black-skinned youth will tend to group themselves together and the white-skinned youth will tend to group themselves together. Most times, they will arrange themselves together based on their physical appearances and features. It is human nature to gravitate to the group you think best reflects you.

One of the reasons we do this is because we tend to feel comfortable with ourselves and when we are in an unfamiliar situation or with people we don't know, we want to feel comfortable. For the most part, we feel comfortable with ourselves, so we tend to gravitate towards people who we perceive to be similar to us. People who are more like us physically, we reason, will understand us easier and reduce our feelings of anxiety. So it just makes sense that we tend to naturally want to be with people who we think are similar to us. It decreases our internal resistance, and we perceive that it will produce less stress and work.

The only challenge is that many times we only take into consideration our external appearance – what we look like on the outside and not who we are on the inside. Our outer appearance can give us superficial information – visual cues that many times are not accurate because they are not complete. Based solely on our skin colors, the appearance of our bodies, and its functional capacity, we can make an overall determination of what cultural groups others belong in, but that information is not entirely accurate because it is incomplete information. It doesn't give you any information on who we are as human beings - what things we value, are passionate about, gives us joy, who we love, and the list goes on and on.

Our external appearance is one way we consciously and unconsciously exclude others. Our assumptions feed into our unconscious biases. Stereotypes and judgments we make about different cultural groups. When we follow our assumptions, we can automatically exclude others particularly when we haven't really taken the time to get to know them.

> *Every single person is praiseworthy of things you*
> *may not expect; it is difficult for us to see that,*
> *especially when we're so powerfully guided by*
> *the things we expect to be true in the world.*

Personal preferences play an important role in molding our personal culture. For instance, just because I am a black woman, who is over the age of 40, married, living on the East Coast, doesn't mean that I can represent or speak for all the black women who are over the age of 40, who are married, and living on the East Coast. Even though we may have a boat-load of shared aspects, there may be many more distinctive cultural aspects that we differ on that would make us totally different in how we think, act, react and respond in the world: *Religion • Experiences • Family Structure • Financial Status • Education • Moral Code • Values • Traditions • Language • Friends • Extended Family • Food • Health • Lifestyle • Music • Traditions • Beliefs • Physical Function/Capability.*

Our soul crews have been consigned and distributed all across the planet. Our job is to remember them when life reconnects us.

There are over seven billion expressions of Divine Source all across the planet. Members of your soul family will be cleverly disguised in a multiplicity of colorful Earth suits. All different shapes, sizes, colors, ages, and abilities. You will know them (many times) only when you are in close proximity and are engaging with them. There will be a quickening of your spirit, a familiarity, an unspoken knowingness, a joy, a relief. You will feel them and know them when you encounter them. Be on the lookout.

Our vibrations align with our spiritual kinfolk.

I am reminded of many of our superhero movies: *The Avengers, The Fantastic Four, The Justice League,* and *X-Men* to name a few. In each of these hero clusters, none of the superheroes are alike. No two beings are equipped with the exact same capabilities or strengths. It is only when they combine their individual gifts and strengths are they able to defeat their enemies.

It is the same as our soul's crew. Each individual member is there to encourage, to strengthen, to support, and to collaborate with others in their group. You will recognize other members of your soul family not with your physical eyes, but with your spiritual eyes. So, don't get caught up in the appearance of things.

Some members of your soul's family network might not be wearing the same color costume as you. They might be in a different disguise based on the tasks that they came here to accomplish. One may have a vision, another may have resources, another may have negotiation skills, another may be creative, while yet another may be a warrior/protector. There are limitless possibilities, talents, and gifts that members of your soul family have come to this planet to share. Sometimes we can miss out on bonds of friendship that can run deeper than our bloodlines, especially when we expect our soul's kinfolk to look and act just like us.

Sometimes members of our soul family are under deep cover. There are spiritual operatives that are working all across this planet, and you would never even know it by just looking at their outer physical appearance. Many times members of our soul family come through various different wombs at different times, and even in different parts of the world to gain whatever experiences they need. Don't be too quick to prejudge, dismiss or marginalize others' life paths. You never know – what they are learning may be an asset to you (and vise-versa).

With over seven billion expressions of Divine Source currently on the planet, I guarantee you that you will find at least one or two soul family members during any given chapter of your life that gravitate towards you and who don't mirror your experience.

When you get your dream team together, that is when your world will energetically shift. You can definitely have strong biological ties with your family of origin because you share genetic traits. With your soul family, you are sharing spiritual characteristics. There is love, inner-standing, and appreciation that goes beyond words and defies human understanding. When you engage, you will know. Sometimes they are members of your biological family or dominant cultural group only and sometimes you may have a multicultural soul family network. Either way, if the relationships are authentic, trustworthy, respectful and empowering, it's all good. When you know who you are and why you are here, you can then exceed your wildest imaginings.

When our son was about 12 years old, he said a profound thing - just in passing (you know how children can sometimes drop nuggets of wisdom and clarity when we least expect it and are open to receive it). In the midst of eating dinner, Jelani said, *"I know that I am part eagle because I have wings deep down in my soul."* My initial reaction was silent awe. In response, my silent (and of course verbal) prayer is that my son is blessed with the discernment to distinguish between people who also have hidden wings and those who will be envious of his invisible wings because they haven't discovered or uncovered their invisible superpower and gifts buried deep within them. I often remind him that there will be those who are for him and those who are against him and that they will come in all shapes, colors, and sizes.

Sometimes your soul family will be members of your biological family, and sometimes they will be acquaintances or even complete strangers. The key is, once you know who you are and are secure in that knowledge, you will be able to recognize your tribe members by their vibration, how they resonate with your vibration and how they make your soul feel. Members of your soul family may be in your life for a season, a reason, a project, a life class, or a lifetime. They may come just to walk with you through a particular life challenge, be with you while you wait or just accompany you to your next destination. They may come in and out of your life, but the soul ties remain. You'll find that it is easy to pick up right where you left off without feelings of guilt; secure in the knowledge that the connection is real, unbreakable, and eternal.

> *Don't be alarmed by good-byes. A good-bye is*
> *necessary before the next hello. And coming together*
> *again, irrespective of time and space, is inevitable*
> *for those who are spiritual family and friends.*

Keep your soul light burning bright so that your soul family can easily find you. The world needs more super heroes. Don't be a *"Human Being (Bean) Boozled."*

CHAPTER FOURTEEN

✦✦✦✦✦

MUSTERING UP THE ENERGY: WOKE WORK®

*"What kept me sane was knowing that
things would change, and it was a question
of keeping myself together until they did."*
– Nina Simone, musician and civil rights activist

There is an increasingly palpable sense of urgency pervading our world right now. We are experiencing a spiritual cleansing – a cleansing so pure that it's like ice cold water interrupting a peaceful sleep and countless are feeling our collective stirring.

Many are touting the phraseology of "*Woke*," but what does that really mean? In truth, unless you are completely exhausted, it takes minimal effort to wake up. You can even wake up from a coma, but then what? Waking up is just the beginning. There is work that has to be done. Normally when you wake up, if your mental and physical human body is functioning, an action is required. You have to swing your legs to the side of the bed, sit up, and stabilize your feet on the ground. You have to get grounded. Once you have grounded yourself back into this reality, then you stand up and get busy – in motion – with the rest of your day. After "*woke*" comes the real work.

What is the "*Work*" that we have to do? Racism, bias, inequity, prejudice, and cross-cultural division won't magically end just because we discover and understand what they are. There is still much work to do. The work is to dissect and dissolve all of the things that divide us. Not just the things that we can see, but more importantly, the things that we feel.

The number one cause of death in America is heart disease. Our minds can understand the concept of wholeness, but only our hearts and souls can experience it. And the reward – if we can endure the experience – is that we don't just grasp the concept of oneness – we feel and embody it.

Our 'woke' work is Heart Work. Our task is to compassionately deal with the parts of us that we hide behind with masks. Our job is to identify those places within us that divide people into boxes, sorting and ascribing value to them as if they were coins. Our work is to uncover our personal stuck points, trauma, and emotional triggers then lovingly address them. We must work to understand our stories, unconscious biases, and our implicit associations then work to change our own mindsets. Ultimately it is our work because we are the keepers of our own souls. When we do our healing work, the results can then be magnified a thousand times because we then pour all of that new information into the Collective Consciousness.

Through compassion my heart expands to include you and your pain.

Real transformation takes time and energy. Collectively we are experiencing the push-pull of birth. Massive contractions and labor pains that are requiring us to push ourselves beyond our comfort zones to give birth to something new. Often it can feel as if time is moving at a snail's pace when it comes to issues of equity, social justice, and reform. It can be easy to fear that things will remain the same, even as they are changing.

We just can't get caught up in the appearance of things. My son, when he was a pre-teen, used to get frustrated when he couldn't see himself growing. He would measure himself practically every day. He continued to grow even though he couldn't see it. Our world is changing even if we can't see it because we are changing. We leave so much of our personal power untapped and unused because we have become emotionally drained. Our Woke Work® is to shift our consciousness back to the vibration of our Divine Source and then interact with one another from there. Seeing each other through new eyes.

> *"My destination is no longer a place –*
> *rather a new way of seeing."*
> - Marcel Proust, French novelist

Much of our energy is zapped because we hide our emotions. Smiling even when we are in pain because whenever we are asked during a greeting, *"How are you?"* we have come to understand that what most people really want is the canned response *"I'm fine, and how are you?"* even if our heart is aching and we feel sad, tired and overwhelmed. Both young and not so young people are being plagued with thoughts of suicide; both functioning and debilitating depression are more common than we can even imagine. We have created a society where wearing masks to hide our feelings is pretty much expected. Over time, if we haven't fostered safe havens where we can take off our masks and just be ourselves, we wind up stuffing our emotions and eventually drowning in them.

Over the past two decades, what I have found is that most people of all cultures, ethnicities, and backgrounds, want to both talk and heal around this topic, especially if they are in environments that are devoid of shame, guilt, and judgment. They want to heal through processes safely designed to support moving stuck emotional energy in the body. They want to course correct all of the stories that are deeply embedded within... stories that prevent us from deeply connecting to our hearts and souls.

So I, along with a small but effective band of seasoned personal development facilitators, crafted an amazing life-altering opportunity called **Woke Work**®. These processes are designed to specifically address our cultural differences, our individual and collective cellular memories, and to provide tools to help participants gain a foothold in their struggles to understand the ways that racism, unconscious bias, privilege, and prejudice operate in their minds. What I know through my own experience is that you can't heal people, nor can you force enlightenment. But what we can do is set up the conditions where people can safely do their inner transformational work. This is a type of **Woke Work**® that we make available; a dualistic work that accesses both our human and spiritual consciousness.

There is a lot for us to unpack with each other. There are so many that are the walking wounded, drowning in a sea of unresolved emotional baggage. What encourages me is when I witness authentic relationships form out of the raw ingredients of cross-cultural strife, hatred, and even emotional trauma.

Only when we face the darkest side of
our beings is healing possible.

Throughout this book, I hope that you have gained insight and also the courage to look at some of the things that may be keeping you feeling a bit fragmented and disconnected from others. I am encouraged because there is a part of us that isn't broken. The human soul is always looking for a deeper and more meaningful expression of itself. When we are led by our souls, the Divine Source within us always knows what to do to heal the human parts of us. Our **Woke Work**® is to maneuver ourselves past our Representative personas and engage with our Divine Source that is embodied in our VIP (Vibrationally Intelligent Perspective).

Change is inevitable; transformation is optional.

What I know to be true, is that whatever we desire and need from a soulful perspective, is always provided, we just have to keep moving forward and towards our goals. We have to muster up the energy within us. It can be difficult because we carry so much historical baggage within and around us that tells us through countless examples that we are permanently divided. And yet, there are just as many examples of where that is not true, but we can't and won't see it unless we adjust our lenses.

> *"I love because my love is not dependent on the object of love. My love is dependent on my state of being. So whether the other person changes, becomes different, friend turns into a foe, does not matter, because my love was never dependent on the other person. My love is my state of being. I simply love."*
> – Osho, spiritual guru

Healing starts from within and if we can adjust our internal eyesight, what we see, feel, create, and experience externally will be different. We have more power to shape our experiences than we know. One hundred percent of our work is to enhance our receptivity and raise our internal vibration. It has absolutely nothing to do with our skin color and has everything to do with the energy that we are emitting. Our brains and bodies down to the cellular level have to be cleared of all programs, thoughts, beliefs, memories, and internal structures that we have created around the concept of race. It is an inside job and we can heal. When we do our own personal healing work, the world will heal around us.

> *"Love takes off masks that we fear we cannot live without and know we cannot live within."*
> – James Baldwin, American novelist, playwright and activist

For information on Woke Work®, visit *www.WokeWork.org.*

CHAPTER FIFTEEN

THE GREAT REMEMBERING

"All learning is just the soul remembering."
– Plato, philosopher

Excuse me. Haven't we met before? What part of me are you attaching a story to? Are you mixing and matching the remembrance of me? Filling in the blanks with faded memories. I know you. I remember remnants of you. Through my spirit eye, you look just like you did before. Where are you going this time? I want to go! I think there is something that I am not seeing clearly. There is a faint remembrance of something. Something...I did... something you did...something we did. It is all a blur. But I do know you from somewhere. Give me a second...I am beginning to remember.

If you could whisper fifteen things into the heart, mind, and collective ear of humanity, what would you say? Here's what I would say:

1. *"After "woke" comes the real work."*

2. Ease and Flow – We *really* don't have to attend every argument, disagreement, and fight that we are invited to.

3. We can't get to really *"know"* each other if we are covered in protective layers of emotional plastic wrap.

4. Remember that we are souls and that everyone we encounter is a soul as well. Each life we touch helps change the narrative on both sides – either positively or negatively.

5. As we heal individually, we heal the planet. Whatever gifts you share that are from your soul, the planet needs; whether you are an Ambassador, Activist, Teacher, Advocate, Cultural Protector or Keeper. We all lose when you play small.

6. Don't become so obsessed with fear and death that you forget to live. Just because we can't fully remember who we are, doesn't mean we don't have a vibrant spiritual backstory.

7. The internal resistance that we feel when we engage cross-culturally is the last push to denying our oneness.

8. Our greatest challenge is to find the congruence between what we see, what we know, and what we feel, then allowing it to be expressed through each moment of our lives.

9. Don't get caught up in the appearance of things; the world is changing as we all continue to spiritually evolve. And we each experience exactly what we need for our soul's evolution. It is *All Good* (even when we humanly don't quite understand it all).

10. When we truly understand how connected we really are and that we are not the human flesh that covers us, things change.

11. How to make new friends: Be Brave.

12. Whether we remember it or not, we choose our families before we get here to Earth School. We choose the opportunities that are interesting, challenging, and that will afford us the most potential for spiritual growth.

13. Everything you need is already within you. We activate whatever clarity we need when we move from spiritual, social, and ethical neutrality. What we need spiritually is not always what we humanly want.

14. Every now and then, it is a good practice to look inside of yourself to see what parts of you are not getting enough light, love, and energy, then adjust yourself accordingly.

15. Love, that elusive thing called love. We can only give and receive it, not get or take it, so be generous in your giving.

What if life is just about the stories we create and tell? What if we are in the midst of writing the greatest story *being* told – the story of humanity? What if we are just in the prologue of this unbelievably colorful and dramatic epic tale? History will surely repeat itself if we are not careful. So, we will be careful. We will continue to spiral upwards with our universal DNA uniting us as one.

As I muse over the journey of my soul as well as all of our souls, I often wonder, what will be the end to all of this? How will we move our collective cross-cultural dial from fear to love? It will be the moment we remember that within each of us is a spark of Divine Source energy. The very same power that binds us together as humans. With that as our collective common denominator, it would just make sense that we should seek the Divine in everyone we meet.

We will know that we have learned the lessons of this colorful experience when the hues of our Earth suits are no longer in the first sentence of our descriptions of one another. When it is truly an afterthought and not the first thing that we see or will ourselves to *not* see. It will be our souls shining through as they are emanating the color that matches the vibration of our Divine Source.

What Color Is Your Soul? It is a vibration. The color, just like the high-pitched tone of a dog's whistle, vibrates beyond the range of the human ear. We have to raise our vibration to match our Divine Source – the Universal Soul. Once we do, we will realize that, in our humanness, we don't have sufficient color descriptors. There are colors that vibrate way beyond our visual spectrum in their purity. So, what color are our souls? They are the color of the Divine. A color that encompasses everything that is.

When you look into the very depths of me, what is the color that you see?

Is it crimson red from my blood that was shed? Or do you see ghostly hauntings of pale white that caused terror in the night? Perhaps it is the blinding midnight bluish black, as I brailled my way back into yet another lifetime of color? What color will I choose to be this time? Mixing shades to make the perfect masterpiece and disguise. There are millions of colors of me. Like faded signatures on a page, I have left my drawings in various shades to be interpreted and reimagined by the art collectors and curators of time. Scraping the paint off my soul – never quite removing the previous coat. I'll come back with stains from battles fought long ago and with both learned and unlearned lessons scribbled across my soul. What color shall I choose to be this time? I smile, knowing that I have an infinite array to choose from. With eyes closed, I pick one. A cocoa brown. It feels rich and silky smooth. Dangerously consumable. Teaching me the lessons of self-confidence and self-preservation this go round. I will keep choosing until I love them all because they are all the various shades of me. I am a collection of cultures, a cornucopia of inspiration and Divine thought.

I am a part of everything and everything is a part of me.

ABOUT THE AUTHOR

Niambi Jaha-Echols is an Author, Inspirational Speaker, Cultural Agility Strategist, Spiritual Activist and has spent the past 30 years working as a Transformation Advocate. She is the Principal and Lead Consultant for Cross-Cultural Agility, LLC where she trains, coaches and consults individuals and corporations on issues supporting cultural intelligence and new pathways to inclusion.

Niambi's passion is helping others to transform their mindsets and personal stuck points so that they can deepen their connections to all of humanity.

She is the Founder of The Butterfly Movement, which utilizes the symbolism of the caterpillar/butterfly metamorphosis to foster emotional and spiritual transformation in women and girls. Niambi is a co-contributor to the book "African Americans and Community Engagement in Higher Education" published by SUNY Press and is also the author of "Project Butterfly" and "Inspiring the Souls of Our Girls."

She has been featured in Essence and Ebony Magazines, MSN.com and Oprah's Angel Network for her work with teen girls. She is a faculty member of Expert Online Training, is a member of the National Diversity Council and serves as a Professional Advisor to graduate students at DePaul University's School for New Learning. She is also a Program Faculty member of Art of Living Retreat Center in Boone, NC.

What excites her is when she can provide tools to help others gain a foothold in their struggles to understand the ways that racism, unconscious bias, privilege, and prejudice operate in our minds - notably when she can support authentic relationships constructed out of the raw ingredients of cross-cultural differences.

Niambi, her husband and teenaged son lives in traditional Occaneechi territory - now known as Chapel Hill, NC.

BRING NIAMBI TO YOUR BUSINESS, ORGANIZATION OR EVENT

NIAMBI JAHA-ECHOLS
Widening the Circle

Speaker • Author • Spiritual Activist • Facilitator

Niambi knows the importance of choosing the correct speaker. The right one sets the stage for success and the wrong one for disaster. Niambi's authentic approach combined with superb content positions her as a top choice for many businesses and events. She customizes each message and training to achieve and exceed the objectives of her clients.

CONTACT NIAMBI TODAY TO BEGIN THE CONVERSATION.

www.NiambiJaha-Echols.com

You've Read The Book
Are You Ready For The Experience?

Woke Work™
Healing the Illusion of Our Separateness

REFRAME & RECALIBRATE TO THE ROOT

www.WokeWork.org

Join Our Community

Transforming our cultural differences and our
individual and collective cellular memories.

CROSS-CULTURAL HEALING

Raising the World's Vibration, One Self at a Time.

www.CrossCulturalHealing.com

Now that you have read The Story of Akna and Her Children... the journey can continue!

Join Mama Edie Armstrong and friends as they tap into the reservoir of storytelling through original personal stories, multicultural folktales, spiritual and other wisdom stories, reminding us of the amazing connections we all have.

During the curricular study of *"The Story of Akna and Her Children,"* join us as we examine how we became so wounded and what we can do to heal, closing the chasm that often keeps us apart. Discuss with artists, educators, parents and others ways to avoid continued wounding through the podcast, "What Shall I Tell My Children?"

www.OneSameFamily.org

CPSIA information can be obtained
at www.ICGtesting.com
Printed in the USA
FSHW021828300120
66656FS